In our sophisticated society today, our young people are often taught that it is more virtuous to lose gracefully than to win. But there isn't any virtue in losing! The end effect of such teaching is that young people will not be bothered by losing. They won't hurt inside, where it counts. And if it doesn't bother them, they'll be *consistent* losers.

The true competitor is hurt deeply when he loses. He acknowledges his defeat, but he convinces himself it is only temporary and he will come back, and come back, and come back, until he stands in the winner's circle.

We need sportsmanship, true, but let's not misconstrue sportsmanship to mean a casual acceptance of defeat.

Christ is the victory in life. Nobody wins without Christ—nobody.

NO
TIME
FOR LOSING

Francis A. Tarkenton

BALLANTINE BOOKS • NEW YORK

Copyright © 1967 by Fleming H. Revell Company

All rights reserved. Published in the United States by Ballantine Books, a division of Random House, Inc., New York,
and simultaneously in Canada by Ballantine Books of Canada,
Ltd., Toronto, Canada.

Library of Congress Catalog Card Number: 67-22574

ISBN 0-345-25696-4-175

This edition published by arrangement with
Fleming H. Revell Company

Manufactured in the United States of America

First Ballantine Books Edition: November 1976

*To all my teammates
throughout the years*

Contents

Preface

"Football," says Fran Tarkenton, with a twinkle in his eyes, "is *real*. There's nothing theoretical about it. When two or three guys, each weighing 250 pounds or more, jump on you and smash you to the ground, there isn't any doubt in your mind that this is really happening."

This awareness of reality is one of the big reasons Fran Tarkenton handles himself so successfully on the gridiron—and in life. Although this six-footer weighs only 195 pounds—less than average for a pro quarterback—he comes on strong, obliterating an opposing team's defenses, passing when he can, scrambling when he has to, and living up to his reputation as one of the two or three finest quarterbacks in the nation.

To print the public accolades and applause which have greeted this young man throughout his football career—starting in high school where he made the varsity football team in his freshman years—would make another book, twice as long as this one. Wally Butts, the football coach at the University of Georgia, wrote of Fran: "In thirty years in sports, I've never met a finer boy or better leader of men." Sportswriters have called him a "magician" on the field, and one reporter tagged Fran as the best quarterback in the nation while he was still in college. We couldn't begin to quote half the comments about Fran, and, more important, Fran wouldn't let us. That's the other side of Fran Tarkenton . . . the sincere, unassuming side that enables him to come on strong in life and be just as big a champion off the field as on.

Fran Tarkenton is big-boned and rangy. There's nothing dainty about him. He has a rugged, wide-open face that promises a straightforward approach toward any problems that may come his way. When he talks with you, you know immediately that here is an intelligent man, well rounded in his learning and experiences, and undoubtedly one of the warmest, friendliest persons you've ever met. He understands people and likes them and answers questions in a direct, uncomplicated manner that never leaves you in doubt as to his feelings on a subject. This does not mean he is brusk. Just the opposite; he is extremely courteous, soft-spoken and sensitive to the feelings of others. But, through it all, when he's finished talking, the listener knows that Fran has made his points clearly and without compromise.

On the football field, the reality is the goal post. "That's what I'm out there for," says Fran. "To win. There's a misdirection in sportsmanship today. I fear we have given out youth a philosophy of accepting defeat by instructing them to be good losers. There is no virtue in losing. Show me a *good* loser, and I'll show you a *loser*."

In life, to Fran Tarkenton the reality is Jesus Christ. "There isn't any other way to win in life. Through all our efforts and skills and sacrifices in this material world, all we can really have is just the *hope* of victory—and that's not enough. But, in God's great plan for men, He has gone a further step . . . and through His Son, Jesus, He has given us the *promise* of victory!"

These are the realities of which Fran Tarkenton is constantly aware, and his determination to compete against those things which would rob him of victory —in football and in life—has fashioned him into the kind of man of whom one admirer wrote: "If my three boys can grow up to have the character, personality and humility of Francis Tarkenton, then I will feel my life has been a success."

That is a truly great compliment, and it expresses an attitude with which the publishers of this book thoroughly agree.

There's no need for us to say more than that about Fran Tarkenton.

THE PUBLISHERS

Francis Asbury Tarkenton

Led football team of Athens High School to State Championship.

Was selected to All-State football, basketball and baseball teams while at Athens High School.

Led University of Georgia freshman team to unbeaten, untied season; was selected for All-SEC freshman team, in 1957.

Was selected for All-SEC sophomore team at T-QB, in 1958.

Led University of Georgia to SEC Championship (7-0-0 SEC record) and 14-0 victory over Missouri in Orange Bowl, throwing two touchdown passes, in 1959.

Served as Co-Captain, University of Georgia, in 1960.

Was selected for All-American second team (Associated Press), in 1960.

Was selected for All-American Academic first team (major, Business Administration), in 1960.

Won Governor's Trophy as Outstanding Back in Hula Bowl at Honolulu, leading East to 14-7 victory over West, and completing nineteen out of thirty-three passes for 204 yards and two touchdowns, in 1960.

Led SEC in total offense with 1,274 yards, in 1960.

Led SEC in passing with 108 out of 185 (58.4 percent) for 1,189 yards and seven touchdowns, in 1960.

Was named All-Pro quarterback in 1975.

Was named Most Valuable Player in the NFL for 1975.

CAREER PASSING RECORD AT GEORGIA

YEAR	ATTEMPTS	COMPLE-TIONS	INTER-CEPTIONS	YDS. GAINED	TDs	PCT.
1957	26	12	0	107	3	46.2
1958	30	16	2	175	5	53.3
1959	102	62	6	736	6	60.8
1960	185	108	12	1,189	7	58.4
Orange Bowl	16	9	1	128	2	56.2
Totals	359	207	21	2,335	23	57.7

CAREER PASSING RECORD IN NFL

YEAR	ATTEMPTS	COMPLE-TIONS	INTER-CEPTIONS	YDS. GAINED	TDs	PCT.
1961	280	151	17	1,997	18	56.1
1962	329	163	25	2,595	22	49.5
1963	297	170	15	2,311	15	57.2
1964	306	171	11	2,506	22	55.9
1965	329	171	11	2,609	19	52.0
1966	358	192	16	2,561	17	53.6
1967	377	204	19	3,088	29	54.1
1968	337	182	12	2,555	21	54.0
1969	409	220	8	2,918	23	53.8
1970	389	219	12	2,777	19	56.3
1971	386	226	21	2,567	11	58.5
1972	378	215	13	2,651	18	56.9
1973	274	169	7	2,113	15	61.7
1974	351	199	12	2,598	17	56.7
1975	425	273	13	2,994	25	64.2
Totals	5,225	2,931	212	38,840	291	56.1

CAREER RUSHING RECORD IN NFL

YEAR	ATTEMPTS	YDS.	AVG.	LONGEST	TDs
1961	56	308	5.5	52	5
1962	41	361	8.8	31	2
1963	28	162	5.8	24	1
1964	50	330	6.6	31	2
1965	56	356	6.4	36	1
1966	62	376	6.1	28	2
1967	44	306	7.0	22t	2
1968	67	301	5.3	22	3
1969	37	172	4.6	21	0
1970	43	236	5.5	20	2
1971	30	111	3.7	16	3
1972	27	180	6.7	21	0
1973	41	202	4.9	16	1
1974	21	120	5.7	15	2
1975	16	108	6.8	21t	2
Totals	609	3,629	6.0	52t	28

1

A Gathering of Stars

It was August, 1958. I was between my freshman and sophomore years at the University of Georgia. Behind me lay four years as a star in high school football and one season as a quarterback on Georgia's freshman squad. I might have thought I was pretty important, but right at that moment I was a guest at a conference of America's finest athletes in Estes Park, Colorado, and just by looking around the room I knew what a long, tough road I'd have to climb before I could take my place among this elite group.

Allie Reynolds, Otto Graham, George Kell, Bud Wilkinson . . . these were some of the great sports figures I was rubbing elbows with. It was a humbling experience. And needless to say, it was one of the most exciting moments of my life. Georgia's assistant football coach, Cal Stoll, had worked a few miracles to get four football players from the university to this conference. Tommy Lewis, Charlie Britt, Tommy Paris and myself—all quarterbacks—were the lucky ones to be chosen, and I believe we would have walked to Colorado if necessary. (We didn't. We flew.)

The conference was to last a week, and all of us looked forward to meeting the athletes we'd idolized for years. I don't know what we expected, but we knew it was going to be sports, sports, sports. And, as far as I was concerned, that was about the only subject in the world worth talking about.

Estes Park must be one of the most beautiful spots in the world. Nestled at the foot of the Rocky Mountains, the park had formerly been a rendezvous for Indians and traders in the early 1800's, and was selected partly because its beauty and tranquility affected all who saw it and enabled trading to proceed in a friendlier, more productive fashion. It certainly had an inspiring effect on me, and when opening night of the conference arrived, and I took my seat in the huge outdoor auditorium, surrounded by the magnificent peaks of the Rockies, I somehow knew I was about to enter into one of the greatest experiences of my life. I had no inkling what it was going to be, and, when it came, it was totally unexpected.

Bud Wilkinson was the first speaker of the evening . . . and that's when an unlooked-for chain of events began to happen.

To put it honestly, athletics and football were the most important part of my life throughout my four years in high school. When I scored a touchdown, and the fans yelled, and I saw my name and picture in the newspapers . . . well, this was the life. This was all I wanted.

As far as my religion was concerned, it was important and meaningful to me, but, as with many boys of high school age, it had receded somewhat into the background. Every morning before breakfast—before one bite had been taken—our family would read Scripture and have a devotional, asking for God's help and guidance during the coming day. In the evenings, I would close my day with a prayer of thanks for God's companionship.

In addition to this constant awareness of God in my life, I also attended church regularly . . . on Sunday, and then again at a midweek service. I didn't drink or smoke and I watched my language carefully. In short, I showed all the outward signs of being a

Christian, and I was perhaps more aware of Christ in my life than most boys . . . but something was missing. My faith was static. It wasn't vital and alive, and I can think of it only as being bottled up within me.

One of the problems in those days was that none of my good friends belonged to my fundamental denomination. The truth is, my religion often made me self-conscious. It was sinful for us to go to movie shows, for example, and this would invariably cause my friends to raise their eyebrows. To an impressionable teen-ager, such reactions can be disturbing, and they disturbed me. This wasn't so much because others didn't accept my religion—I've never been one to worry about such things—but because I *also* felt the same way about my conservative teachings. There was always a gnawing belief within me that Christianity is a lot more than a bunch of "don't" rules, and that there were probably a lot of other fellows walking around, doing things I didn't who were perhaps closer to Christ than I was. This factor, more than anything else—this constant doubt and questioning of my fundamental teachings—made me dissatisfied with my religion and unhappy with myself. I didn't stray from Christ, but knowing His will more fully was a deep need within me.

These are some of the reasons why I say my faith had receded a little during my high school years. I was confused and needed something to straighten me out . . . I needed a new dimension to my faith, a new awakening.

And, as you can see, my thoughts about God were troubled and hazy when I waited for Bud Wilkinson to begin talking that night in 1958 in Estes Park, Colorado.

The one aspect of this athletic conference which had not really registered on me was that all the speakers were members of the Fellowship of Christian Athletes. This had been explained to me briefly, but my interest in attending, of course, lay along other lines, and whatever it was I expected to hear from Bud Wilkinson, it certainly wasn't what he talked about.

Bud stood on the platform in front of the microphone, the audience hushed, and he witnessed quietly and reverently to the miracle of Christ working in his life. He spoke of Christian faith and what it meant to him. And although I was not too surprised to hear some talk about Christ at the conference, I was spellbound by the emphasis placed upon Him and by the obvious sincerity in Bud's voice and manner.

During that week, Bud was followed by many speakers . . . big, strong, fine-looking athletes, some of the roughest and toughest men in the world . . . and all witnessed unashamedly to the power and joy of Christ in their lives and careers. Many of the speakers weren't polished, but there was no mistaking their sincerity. All of them were great successes in sports, and yet the most important thing in the world to them was their God—and they had come here, to Estes Park, to tell others about it.

I was particularly impressed with the sheer *guts* it must have taken for these men to stand up in front of that huge audience and speak of their faith so bluntly. Never in my life have I spent a more inspiring and astounding week.

After I had been in Estes Park three or four days, Don Meredith (now the quarterback for the Dallas Cowboys), Henry Christopher, an end for Southern Methodist, and the four of us from the University of Georgia started hiking up one of the nearby mountains. About half-way up, Henry and I suffered a mutual attack of asthma or bronchial congestion—nothing serious, but uncomfortable enough to make us decide to stay where we were while the other fellows went to the top.

As I sat there, catching my breath, conscious of the immense beauty of these mountains and the utter quiet and natural splendor surrounding us, I reflected on the testimonies I'd heard and I was more than ever aware of my own inadequacies. I was always self-conscious when asked to speak of my faith, and it was the furthest thought from my mind to ever initiate a religious discussion. It was all too clear to me that I was hiding my faith under a rock, and I even wondered if perhaps I wasn't a little ashamed, on occasion, of admitting I was a Christian. It was an intense moment of soul-searching, and I didn't like what I found.

Then I prayed. I prayed hard and sincerely that day for God to give me strength to always witness for Jesus Christ—to set aside the fears and doubts and technicalities of "do's" and "don'ts," and to witness to the power and love of Christ as I had seen these men do. I wanted this strength more than anything else I had ever wanted in my life, including football, and I knew I had to honor my faith and serve my Lord at whatever cost.

It was a total rededication of my life to Christ, and it was the deepest emotional experience I've ever had. It was that new dimension I had been seeking.

It can truthfully be said that when I returned from Estes Park, I returned as a new man. The faith that had always been within me, and the many seeds that had been planted early in my life, began to bear fruit. Never again did I step out on a football field without being very much aware that I was not alone. I had an ally in Christ—not that this meant I would always win, but I knew I would always be able to do my best. Never again did I make a major decision, or face a tough problem, or suffer defeat alone. Christ was, and is, within me as a constant companion. And never again did I consciously step back from witnessing to my faith at any time it was possible.

And, if there is a secret common to the success of those fine young men who have banded together in the Fellowship of Christian Athletes, now you know what it is.

2

Back-Alley Workouts

I was ten years old before I became involved in any kind of organized sports. Until then, all my sports activities were strictly of the sandlot variety. There was no Little League, or special clubs, or anything like that, and even between the ages of ten and twelve I still spent a good deal of time in spontaneous and unorganized sports.

I feel strongly that informal sports activities are good for young boys. They're uncomplicated, pure fun, and give youngsters a chance to pick and choose the plays, positions and techniques which they enjoy the most and are naturally best at. Any boy who begins his sports life this way can develop a very real love for his game. The pressures of organized programs—at least for very young boys—can sometimes do more harm than good to their athletic futures. Baseball isn't much fun to an eight-year-old when he makes a bad play in front of a hundred people, or lets his team down in a crucial moment. The instinctive love he might have had for the sport, and the fun he had playing it—which is so important to steady progress—is diminished in such pressure-type situations, and I'm glad I didn't have to face problems like this when I was just developing my feelings for sports.

My interest in sports started in Richmond, Virginia, where I was born and lived for the first five years of my life. Even in those days, I can remember playing ball with my father, or my older brother, Dallas—or, for that matter, anyone who would come to the house and be taken in by the pleading look on my face. Daddy served a church in Richmond, and I remember one week we entertained four or five student evangelists. I don't know how much evangelizing they did, but I can certainly vouch for their sports-mindedness. Daddy will attest to this day that the living room was turned into a miniature sports stadium every night after church services.

My entire early life, of course, was deeply imbedded in the church, and all my friends and all my memories of those early days are entirely church-connected. Daddy accepted a pastorate in Washington, D.C., when I was five; I can remember at least two times in the next few years when all of the family accompanied him on his summertime preaching excursions. He'd be asked to preach for ten days in a distant city and we made a family vacation out of it.

These preaching assignments were at the real old-time camp meetings . . . with good music, good preaching, sawdust on the floor . . . and these people really enjoyed their religion. It was fun to them and it meant something. In Oklahoma City, I remember the people bringing their tents and trailers and camping out on the meeting grounds for the full week, or two weeks, of the revival. Preaching would begin at breakfast, break for lunch, resume in the afternoon, break for supper, then really get going in the big evening sessions. Everybody thoroughly enjoyed every minute of it, and they enjoyed their faith in a wonderful way.

These were great days, and I loved them . . . driving around the country in our 1947 Nash, seeing new places, and being part of the great happiness and good cheer which literally rocked the ground in those grand, old-style camp meetings.

In many ways, I will always miss them.

When we moved into our new home in Washington, my brother and I discovered an alley behind our house that quickly became our "gridiron." Rounding up a couple of other fellows, we'd play two-man touch football every chance we got, and I suspect that if we added up all the time we spent in that alley for the next six years it would amount to well over a thousand hours. We were out there every chance we had, rain or shine, hot or cold.

Today, of course, I'm called the "Scrambler," and I really believe that our football games in that narrow, confined alley contributed a tremendous amount to my career. To move in that alley, and to dodge or get off a pass, demanded quickness and a critical sense of direction. When I started becoming a more polished player in high school and college, I brought these vital instincts with me. No matter how another team may crowd me today, it's still a wide-open friendly field to me compared to that spaghetti-thin alley back in Washington.

Another important factor that contributed a great deal to my early development in sports was the simple fact that Dallas was about three years older than I was. He was bigger, stronger, faster, smarter . . . everything I wanted to be. When we played sandlot games of baseball, basketball, or football, most of the players would usually be Dallas' friends and I guess I spent all of my earliest days in sports stretching to be as good or better than boys three or four years older than I was.

Later, when I was ten and joined the Merrick Boys' Club in Washington, I was the youngest member on their 80-pound football team. They put me at end and I never experienced any particular problems playing against older fellows from other clubs.

The same was true for baseball and basketball at the Merrick Boys' Club. I was a forward in basketball and a shortstop in baseball, and, again, I believe I was the youngest member on any of these teams.

Of course, I practiced sports every chance I got, and I must admit that my schoolwork suffered. Somehow, I managed to muddle through my studies, but if I had it to do over again I would balance things out a little better. Even then I was dreaming of a life in sports, and it wasn't until I was maturing in high school that I realized how important good study habits and school marks are to anyone contemplating an athletic scholarship and professional ball. It would have been a lot easier on me if I had developed these study habits in the beginning.

To emphasize the inordinate love I had for sports, I collected football cards from bubble-gum packages and, on those days when the weather was too inclement for even me to go out and practice, I'd spread the cards out on the floor and construct offensive and defensive teams and "play" football. My cards were pictures of professional players, and I found it necessary to learn a lot about each of these men, and their capabilities and techniques, before I could improvise All-Star teams that really made sense. The combinations were endless, of course, and one of the challenges was to put together two teams of almost equal power. With this as a beginning, I'd construct plays and counter-defenses, mastering first one team, then the other, and even I didn't always know beforehand who would win the contest.

This hobby of mine made me a student of football, demanding that I learn a great deal about the rules and other technicalities of the game. Needless to say, my regular school studies again took a back seat to this major interest.

I enjoyed myself so much at this game that even when I was in high school, and my interest had shifted to college football, I was still collecting bubble-gum cards of college players. Years later, when I got into professional ball, I played against several of the men whose pictures I had formerly moved around on the floor. I think I knew as much about them as they knew about themselves.

At one time, during my rookie year with the Vikings, I actually played *with* Hugh McElhenney . . . one of the college stars whose picture I'd collected in high school. Here I was, with a strange feeling I'd gone through all this before, calling plays for him and asking the kind of expert performance from him I'd insisted on back in my living room ten years earlier!

Sportswriters have often asked me if I ever got into any trouble as a young boy—and the answer is no.

Frankly, I didn't have time to get into trouble. I was much too busy with sports and didn't have much chance to think of other ways to use up my energies.

In the last few years we were in Washington, our home was six blocks from the Capitol, a trouble-torn area where gang wars and race problems were daily occurrences. So, it wouldn't have been hard to find trouble if I'd wanted it.

But—and I'm very thankful for this—the only thing I was concentrating on in those days was sports, and any boy who feels the same way, and is serious about becoming proficient in his sports, loving every minute he can play and practice it, will find it very hard to get into trouble. In the first place, he'll *resent* anything that would take up so much time and be so useless. Any boy who has an urge to pick up a knife or a rock, or to double up his fists, ought to pick up a football instead, or a basketball or baseball, and this is one area in which I think organized sports for young boys is beneficial. I indicated earlier that I don't think organized sports programs for the very young will necessarily develop good athletes . . . but, for thousands of youngsters who wouldn't be top athletes anyway, these programs do help to keep them occupied and interested in wholesome activity.

The real answer to this old problem of organized sports versus unorganized sports is like many others in life. A youngster who is determined to be a fine athlete in a given sport will bust his way up through granite no matter what happens. He'll automatically play more sandlot ball than any other kind, regardless of how many clubs he belongs to, because he'll be too impatient to wait for scheduled activities—and he'll practice whenever and wherever he can. If I am ever fortunate enough to have a boy of my own, and if he takes a serious interest in sports, I wouldn't want him to join an organized sports program until he was at least ten or eleven years old. If, on the other hand, he had only an average interest in sports, then I think it might be healthy for him if organized sports occupied at least part of his time.

One final point I'd like to make in this chapter while I'm recalling those early years in Richmond and Washington, is the *age* at which I think a boy should start to tackle a sport seriously if he wants to be a professional player.

That age is *before ten years old*—and I emphasize it.

The younger a boy is, the more able he is to learn and develop. He's willing to risk failure; to try new things; and he won't be discouraged by his lack of proficiency, but will keep coming back, and coming back, and coming back. More important, he will be doing all of this in the years before people are watching him, or booing him, or before he has to make a team and face unpleasant pressures that can destroy his enthusiasm for the game.

A strong competitive spirit is essential, and a boy is more apt to have it at a younger age—while he's still dreaming and hoping and young enough to believe (and understand, because it's true) that nothing will stop him if he keeps trying. As he gets older, some of that dream may be knocked out of him by life, but by then he may just be good enough in his sport to *make* his dream come true.

So—start young. And don't tell me about Cazzie Russell, one of the great basketball players of all time, who didn't even pick up a basketball until he was eleven. Cazzie is the exception that proves the rule.

And—as he testifies so eloquently to all who will listen—Jesus Christ is a very vital part of his life.

3

The Real Beginning

My father left his pastorate in Washington, D.C., in June of 1951. He had recently been awarded a Bachelor of Science degree by Wilson Teachers College (now District of Columbia Teachers College) and he wanted to pursue postgraduate studies at the University of Georgia in Athens. He had considered a number of universities, but he felt that the University of Georgia offered him the best opportunity to further his academic and religious studies.

Daddy's always had something of the pioneer in him, and when the five of us (my little brother, Wendell, had been born in 1947) packed up and headed for Athens, Daddy didn't have a pastorate waiting for him and he had no idea of exactly how he was going to make a living for us. We had some money saved —not much—but it was enough to keep us going for a while, and when we added in our family's never-say-die spirit, well, we had everything we needed. And that was one thing our family really had—spirit and faith. I admit that I had some misgivings about leaving Washington at that particular time, because I'd been selected to play on the All-Star Metropolitan Washington Baseball Team. The game was to be televised and was scheduled to be played at Old Griffith Stadium—one week *after* we all climbed in the car for the move to Georgia! It was a big disappointment

13

for me, but I knew the importance of my daddy's decision and I was as determined as everyone else in the family to take my share of responsibility and help make our new life in Athens run as smoothly as possible. (Anyhow, I *hope* that's the way I felt, because I sure was upset at missing out on that baseball game!)

I want to be certain I don't leave the impression that the Tarkenton family was in any way deprived. Not at all. Money was always meager, as it is in most ministers' families, but we never lacked for good food and warm clothing. Daddy was a good provider, seeing to it that we had all of the material things we really needed, while, at the same time, never compromising the really important matter of spreading the Word of God as best he was able. There was a determination and a purpose about him that must have impressed the leaders in his church considerably, because it wasn't long after we arrived in Athens that Daddy was offered the pastorate of a local church. The salary was low, but a parsonage went with it, helping our financial situation tremendously. Dallas and I helped out in every way we could, and Daddy was always busy on articles and books and, of course, he accepted many preaching missions. All in all, things in Athens worked out very well, right from the start, and no town in the world could have been a better place for me to be brought up—as I was to find out.

The YMCAs I'd been exposed to in Washington—and many others I've since visited, especially in the North—seem to me to be dedicated more to men than to boys. But the YMCA in Athens, Georgia, was almost totally dedicated to young men, and it was here that I met Cobern Kelley, the man who, next to my father, was to have the greatest influence on my early life, both in religion and athletics. Many men, such as "Pop" Pearson, the Executive Secretary of the YMCA, a wonderful Christian leader of boys, contributed greatly to my growth in those days, but Cobern Kelley stands out like a giant.

Kelley (as we called him) was a bachelor. His life was completely dedicated to boys between the ages of 6 and 18, and because he was plainly and simply one of the most *genuine* men ever put on this earth, no boy who spent more than fifteen minutes with Kelley could have walked away without feeling a little warmer toward the human race, happier to be alive, and thinking a little more seriously about the religion that could produce such a fine person.

Kelley was Athletic Director at the Athens YMCA, and he made me aware for the first time that athletics and religion can be combined. Until then, I had always thought of religion as being apart from sports —something for the home or church. But Kelley changed all that with a really unique physical training program.

I joined the Athens YMCA in September of 1951. That was the start of football season, of course, and I reported for practice one afternoon.

"What happens first?" I asked a teammate.

"A half hour of scrimmage," he said.

"Then what?"

"Well, then we go inside and wrestle on the mats for half an hour."

"After that, I guess we get showered up and go home, huh?"

"Nope," said my friend. "We take the showers, all right, but then we have a half hour of Bible study."

I must have looked perplexed, because my friend evidently figured he had to explain it to me. "Look," he said. "Our training sessions are an hour and a half. Kelley says the Bible study is just as important as scrimmage and wrestling."

"For *football?*" I said.

"For football, softball and basketball," he said. "That's the way it is here. You'll get used to it."

Well, we had a pretty good scrimmage that day, with a few good bruises shared by all, and then we went to the mats and tried to wrestle each other's brains out. Next thing we knew, we'd had our showers, and, still glaring at each other from our recent competitive actions, we sat down quietly for Kelley to begin his Bible study.

Kelley walked into the room, stood there looking at us for a few moments, then said: "It makes my heart pound with joy to see how much you all love each other."

Needless to say, we all had a good laugh and it cleared the air of any bad feelings we might have carried in with us from the football field or wrestling mats. More important, it served to show us that no matter how hard we competed in sports, we were still brothers in Christ and could sit down as a team and find the Lord together.

This was the first of many lessons that Kelley taught me. Christ was the most important thing in Kelley's life, and he wanted to be sure we brought Christ into our lives, *fully*—in sports as well as anywhere else. It wasn't that he wanted us to get out there on the field and pat the other fellow's cheek. Not at all. The object in sports is to win . . . to play hard, play fairly, and to give your all to winning. But, if you forget your Christian principles, you can get all wrapped up in bitterness and anger and that is positively the surest way to eventual defeat.

"Balance," Kelley used to say . . . "Balance is the important thing. Remember your God and your religion when you're out there on the field and you'll be able to take every defeat and win right in stride."

Any boy headed for an athletic career is halfway there if he can remember and apply that philosophy. I know.

Of course, it wasn't all hearts and flowers with Kelley. He was a powerhouse of a man and he knew his sports, and aside from instilling us with Christian principles, he worked without letup to turn us into athletes. Thanks to my back-alley training in Washington, I easily made the 11-year-old football team, and in fact, did so well that I soon got to thinking of myself as being the whole team. I was really impressed with myself. I was bigger and better than the other boys, and when we'd play other Y's I'd really figure it was Francis Tarkenton versus the other team, as, indeed, lots of people used to say. But not Kelley. He wasn't impressed a bit, and he had another important lesson in store for me.

We were playing an inter-squad game one night —against a team that was supposed to be a lot tougher than ours—and I was in the tailback slot. Without exaggeration, I believe I made a touchdown for every two times I carried the ball. I mean we really slaughtered that other team, and nobody was more cocky about it than I was.

Kelley didn't say anything that night, but when we went into our next game, Kelley played me at guard, and tackle, and sometimes at end . . . in every position except tailback. He wasn't going to give me a chance to run with the ball, or throw it, or to be any kind of a star at all.

I was sore for a while, but it was the greatest thing that could have happened to me, because it taught me that football is a team game, people working together, and that no man can be a star without a good team supporting him. I think that from that moment forward I really began to understand what athletics were all about and I progressed much more rapidly as a result of having had my horns pulled in when my ego threatened to get out of control.

Kelley worked on me in various ways during my eleventh and twelfth years, always tempering my sports progress with wholesome Christian teachings. I played basketball and softball for the YMCA, and as I grew more proficient, becoming captain of one of the basketball teams and pitcher for the "Sluggers," I never had to be reminded that a lot of other teammates were making my "starring" roles possible.

I was enrolled in the Childs Street School in Athens when I was eleven, and my teacher was Mrs. Jim Whatley. This was fortunate, because the following spring, when I was playing softball during a recreation period, she mentioned it to her husband who just happened to be the Head Baseball Coach (and Assistant Football Coach) at the University of Georgia. He was starting up Athens' first Little League baseball team and he needed a pitcher. Thanks to Mrs. Whatley, he scouted me on the softball field and signed me on as pitcher for the Little League team. It was a very good year. We took the championship and I believe we won every game in which I pitched. One of my teammates was Billy Gambrell, now a star flankerback for the St. Louis Cardinals.

That fall, my brother Dallas and I played on Cobern Kelley's Scorpion Football Team—Dallas at halfback and myself at quarterback. This was the "big dog" team of the YMCA where all of the players, like Dallas, were older than I. As a matter of fact, we played local high school junior varsity teams, and although it seemed we were beaten frequently, Kelley said it was one of the best years the YMCA had enjoyed.

Playing for the Scorpions also gave me my first real taste of personal publicity. In a game with Toccoa High School junior varsity, I was able to complete 10 of 15 aerials for 165 yards. Because of this, and the fact that I was the youngest and smallest member of the team, the *Athens Banner-Herald* gave me a good write-up, referring to me as "Cobern Kelley's cannon-armed 12-year-old Scorpion quarterback."

"How about that," I said to Kelley, showing him my new press clippings.

"Go show it to all the bruised up guards," he said, bringing me down to earth. "I'm sure they'd like to know how well they protected you."

Kelley was proud of me, and he showed it in many ways, but he was equally proud of every member of the team, and it was this Christian philosophy of fairness and humbleness that he wanted me to combine with my natural talent for sports. "You'll be a failure without it," he said to me many times . . . and because

I learned that lesson again and again from Cobern Kelley, I've been able to reach heights in sports that I just couldn't have attained otherwise.

Kelley's direct influence on me was to be a little less in the next four years. I was turning thirteen and starting my freshman year in high school where I was given a berth as alternating quarterback on the varsity football team. There wouldn't be too much time for YMCA programs.

And, during these years, I was to ignore some of Kelley's wise teachings, much to my regret. It took the Fellowship of Christian Athletes' Convention in Estes Park to bring his philosophies back to me and cement them in place forever . . . but that was still four years away and all I could think of now was doing my part to give Athens the best football, basketball and baseball teams in the state of Georgia.

Even Kelley would have agreed with that goal, because my first concern now was for the team and the school.

And some great days were coming up.

4

Learning the Hard Way

Let me skip ahead a minute to professional football.

In 1961—with eight years of high school and college football experience behind me—Norm Van Brocklin put me into my first professional game. It was an exhibition game against the Dallas Cowboys in Sioux Falls, South Dakota, and Van Brocklin decided to launch my pro career by sending me in as quarterback in the final quarter.

In the first drive I was in, I threw a 50-yard touchdown pass to Don Ellerscik. This was the only touchdown made by the Vikings in the game and I had brought it off easily, just as though I were back in college. I really couldn't understand why people said professional ball was so tough. I didn't even have any mud on me.

The next week we played the Baltimore Colts—in Baltimore—and of all the football teams I respected, the Colts were on top of the list. At that time, the Colts were really in their heyday, with players like Johnny Unitas, "Big Daddy" Lipscomb, Gino Marchetti, and many others. Some of the confidence I'd gained in the first game with the Cowboys wavered when I realized I might be playing against the Colts, and I was relieved when Van Brocklin named George Shaw as the starting quarterback.

I sat it out on the bench, contentedly, until somewhere in the middle of the second quarter Van Brocklin decided the offense wasn't doing what he wanted it to do, so he pulled Shaw out and sent me in.

I didn't know what play to call, but, for some reason, the "Screen Pass" popped into my head, which is a play that invites the opposing team in on the passer. The Colts had a good pass defense and I figured the Screen Pass was as good strategy as any. Anyway, it was the only thing I could think of, so I called it, came up to the line of scrimmage and started rattling off the numbers. I remember looking over the line at Gino Marchetti, the big 89, and wondering how anybody could have ever grown so huge, and I admit I was nervous. Scared might even be a better word.

When the snap came and I got the ball, I dropped back like Van Brocklin had told me, faked a pass to my left, retreated two or three more steps, letting the defensive linemen come in on me, then dropped a pass out to Mel Triplett, my fullback on the right.

Triplett caught the ball, and I stood there congratulating myself for having completed a pass against the Colts, admiring my Screen Pass strategy and telling myself how great I was . . . when all of a sudden, Billy Ray Smith, a defensive tackle for Baltimore, drove up on me like a runaway locomotive, creasing the bridge of my nose and knocking me flat on the ground while blood poured out of my face like a fountain.

Next thing I knew, I was being toted off the field and draped across a chair on the sidelines. Cold towels were being put on me and there never was a time in my career when I needed more sympathy. I really wasn't at all sure this was what I wanted to do in life and I thought picking cotton in Georgia might be a little easier.

About this time, Van Brocklin ambled over . . . a crusty old veteran of eleven NFL wars . . . and looked down at me and laughed and said: "Welcome to the NFL, kid."

The reason I tell that story at this point in the book is because I did the same stupid thing in my first high school game . . . just stood there after making a handoff, congratulating myself, and then getting slammed to the ground for my foolishness. This game was against Fulton High School, a bigger school than Athens and with a really tough football team. They were beating us that night, and the coach put me in during the fourth quarter.

On the first call I had, I handed the ball off to my left on a quick dive play, and then just stood around, not doing anything. This was my first game, and my first play in high school ball, and I guess I wanted to see what was going to happen.

Well, something happened all right. One of Fulton's big defensive men came in and . . . you know the rest.

Unlike that first experience in professional ball, however, I was so excited and full of adrenalin that night against Fulton, somebody would have had to hit me with a sledge hammer to put me out of commission.

The only thing that bothers me about it is that I had to learn this lesson twice: a football field is no place for a quarterback to be just standing around, admiring himself or the view!

Even though I was big for my age at thirteen, and had survived many a rough-and-tumble football game, Daddy was concerned about my being put on the varsity football squad. I'd be playing against boys a lot older than I was, and a lot heavier and tougher. Daddy felt that junior varsity might be a better berth for me, but the head coach, Weyman Sellers, convinced my father that I was old enough physically and mentally to make the varsity team. I'm sure Daddy still had some doubts about it, but he knew my desire to make the varsity—quite an honor for me at that age—and he gave his consent. No young athlete could have had a better father than I did, and although there were many times when he was obviously concerned about my welfare, he'd never put his foot down unless I was plainly getting into something really dangerous.

Weyman Sellers was the hardest, toughest coach I've played under. He'd gained his experience under Wally Butts at the University of Georgia, probably the finest coach in football, and certainly one of the most demanding. Weyman Sellers learned well from Butts and he was relentless in his training and in his insistence on bringing out the very best a player had to offer. No coach has ever made me run more, or hit more, and although it was hard at the time, and I often resented the Spartan routine, it was tremendously helpful in my athletic development.

Sellers had seen me play football for the YMCA and he alternated me at quarterback with Bobby Towns and Donald Carnes, Donald was moved to halfback in the first part of the season, so Bobby (a sophomore) and I split up the quarterbacking chores pretty evenly for the remainder of the season.

Coach Sellers was responsible for teaching me the basics of Split "T" quarterbacking. I already knew a great deal about the *game* of football—and I was to learn a lot more, of course—but Coach Sellers saw me as a quarterback and he concentrated on teaching me everything he knew about this particular position. Although I could go back in my files and relate all the games I played in that freshman year, the fact that sticks out most strongly is that this was the year I learned to be a quarterback, and I can only recall it as a year of solid learning and training.

I'm not a particularly fast runner and I don't punt well. So Sellers' original conclusion was that I couldn't be a tailback type of football player. But I could pass and I was a good ball handler, so Sellers put me under center.

Hour after hour, until I thought I would get sick of the whole thing, Sellers made me practice on how to take the snap and follow the center so I wouldn't fumble. It sounds like a small thing, but, to this day, I very seldom fumble a ball, and I believe it may be because I can still see Weyman Sellers watching me out of the corner of his eye and demanding perfection in this most fundamental of all quarterback actions.

Also, he worked with me on moving and working my way down the line of scrimmage. He disciplined me to carry out my fakes and use good ball-handling techniques until I was deceptive enough to fool anybody. There was just never any letup, and even in my senior year Coach Sellers would have our teams practicing sometimes as much as three or four hours a day. He was one of the most determined men to win I've ever known, and if there was one thing he didn't want, it was a good football team; he wanted the *best* football team in the state of Georgia. Well, that suited my sentiments exactly, and before I finished high school, Weyman Sellers was going to get exactly what he wanted—a team that was recognized not only as the best in Georgia, but also hinted at by sportswriters as perhaps the best in the nation!

And the credit belongs 100 percent to Weyman Sellers. He earned it.

Making the varsity team was another lucky break for me in my freshman year, and I played guard. Again, I was the youngest member of the team, and the fellows I played with, and against, were sophomores, juniors and seniors. My brother Dallas, a junior, was on the same team with me at center, and we were referred to as the brother basketball act. (Dallas was actually with me on the football, basketball and baseball teams during my freshman and sophomore years at Athens, which is probably the best reason I did so well . . . just trying to stay up with him.)

We had a great basketball season, winning the Regional Championship in Covington, Georgia, but losing out in the state play-offs to Campbell of Fairburn.

As a freshman, it was a thrill to be a starter on the varsity team, and even more so when we took the Regional Title—a feat nobody thought we'd accomplish. We'd lost ten of our twelve players in the previous year, my brother Dallas and Chester Leathers, being the only returning starters. Hubert Bradley, George Guisler and myself filled out the starting list and all of us really had to work hard to keep our team in contention.

I scored 20 points in the final game of the season and even though I won a few awards, I knew that basketball was really not my game. I wasn't tall enough, and I realized this would be a weak point if I planned to take up the game seriously.

That brings up an important point . . . I've always felt that Dallas was a better athlete than I was, whether in football, baseball or basketball. Dallas was a tremendous offensive fullback and equally as good as a defensive halfback. He had power and great speed and he could have gone almost anywhere in whatever sport he chose. But Dallas didn't have the want . . . the yearning . . . for sports as I did. He wasn't completely dedicated to athletics, and when he went on to college he stayed out of sports almost completely.

It was a case, really, of perhaps a less talented player (myself) going further in the long run because my desires were channelled more purposefully. My determination and tremendous desire to be as good an athlete as possible demanded practice and concentration and eventually resulted in the abilities I have today. I think any boy interested in sports—or any other career—should ask himself just how serious he is, and if he's really dedicated, then he's got a lot going for him that will help him attain his goal.

I started on the varsity baseball team as a freshman, pitching most of the time, but occasionally playing shortstop. Dallas was our left fielder. I believe I pitched one no-hitter that year, and our team went on to win our Regional Championship as we had in basketball. I lost a 1-0 heartbreaker in the opening game for the North Georgia Class A Baseball Championship, and I felt so badly about it that I can still remember to this day that I didn't have any appetite for breakfast the next morning. Billy Henderson, my baseball coach, and a man who was very important to me in those early years, did his best to console me and helped me realize a few important truths.

First of all, I realized that no matter how hard I might play to win, there will inevitably be some losses, and I had better be prepared to take them without bitterness or discouragement (Kelley's old admonition). Secondly, I made up my mind never to accept a loss, and always to refuse sympathy. What was important, was to go back and train harder, play harder, and turn a former loss into a future win. I did this several times in my high school and college career, helping our team win over an opponent that had defeated us earlier, but I believe that particular baseball game brought these philosophies home to me for the first time.

When the baseball season was over that year, I was invited to be a cabin assistant at the Athens YMCA camp in Tallulah Falls, Georgia. "Pop" Pearson ran the camp, assisted by Mike Castronis and Frank Inman, both Georgia high school football coaches. The camp period lasted eight weeks and offered us good fun and fellowship. Aside from hiking, canoeing, swimming and other camp activities, there were hymn singing, inspirational "hours," and group participation in many religious sessions. I enjoyed the camp tremendously, especially because of "Pop" Pearson, but I still had the "unfulfilled" feeling in my religious life and my yearning for high school sports was still the biggest thing in my life.

I couldn't wait to get back and start football practice for my sophomore year.

5

A Promise Made

My football activities in my sophomore year repeated the pattern of my freshman year, although we had a tremendously improved team. Alternating at quarterback with Bobby Towns, now a junior, I did a lot of passing, gradually earning a reputation as a fine high school passer. We had a 9-1 season and clinched the 4-A Regional title. Our next step was a contest with Rockmart High School for the North Georgia Championship, which would give us a crack at mighty Valdosta and the state title.

We played Rockmart on their own football field on a cold December night in 1954. Considering the weather, a big crowd attended the game, including the mayor of Athens and many other dignitaries. The Athens High School football team had come a long way in my sophomore year, and interest in us had grown greatly as we rolled over our competition during the season. There was the possibility of a state title in the wind, and because we were a lower rated school than some of the others we played, statewide attention was focused on us with predictions of an Athens win—which would be a real upset.

At the time in Georgia, the rule book for playoffs for the North Georgia Championship included a provision that if the team wound up with a tie score, the team that had gained the most yards in rushing, passing, and had penetrated the opponent's 20-yard line the most, was awarded the win. It was called "The Penetration Rule," and we were way ahead in this category in the game with Rockmart. My brother Dallas, playing fullback, had run all over the field and must have had at least 100 yards rushing. I'd had a good night, too, connecting with long passes, and there was just no doubt that with the score tied 6-6, and with two minutes left to play in the fourth quarter, we would definitely win this game via the Penetration Rule. It wasn't the way we preferred to win the game, but at least it would be a win and would give us the right to face Valdosta for the big title.

As the final two minutes ticked away, we were on our own 45-yard line and we had a nice little drive going. I called a pass play in the huddle and we went up to the line, hoping we could get a touchdown and take Rockmart on scoring. I faded back after the snap, looking for my receiver and gauging how much time I had left before some of Rockmart's big linemen could come in and get me. My primary receiver was covered, so I chose another target and started to throw the ball. At that instant, I was hit from behind and the ball hit about ten yards in front of me and bounced up in the air.

Well, everybody sort of stood around a moment, and then a Rockmart player picked up the ball and started a wild run for the goal posts. I don't recall that anyone really chased him. I was sure my throw was an incompleted forward pass. So were my teammates, or they would have jumped all over the guy who picked the ball up and ran with it. Even the Rockmart players looked a little surprised as their teammate hotfooted it down the field . . . *but the referee allowed the touchdown!* Rockmart won the game 12-6!

I don't mind admitting that when I got back to the dressing room I sat down and cried like a baby. Never in my life, before or later, did I feel a defeat as much as that one! The whole team was just in a daze, and nothing Weyman Sellers said—or even the mayor of Athens, who came into the dressing room and put his hand on my shoulder, trying to console me—made any difference to us. We were heartbroken.

Sportswriters and spectators were divided on the call, but everyone admitted it was a close decision between a fumble and an incompleted forward pass and that the referee called it as he saw it. I saw films of the game later, and although it definitely looked like my arm was going forward, it was very, very close, and I imagine it would have been impossible for the referee to have made an absolutely accurate decision down there on the field in a split second.

In what I call my "Li'l Book"—a notebook I used to keep to record special things that happened to me —I wrote the following paragraphs about that disastrous night we played Rockmart. You see in these words that I felt personally responsible for the loss, and it was a feeling I just couldn't shake . . . not for a whole year:

> *If someone had dropped a coin, it would have made a resounding noise throughout the dressing room. There was a frequent sob heard somewhere in the room and then a reassuring voice would say, "You did your best."*
>
> *Then, a short, well-built man entered the room quietly. Sobbing stopped for a while and heads of broken-hearted boys began to rise as they recognized the figure to be the backfield coach of the OPPOSING TEAM, Rockmart.*
>
> *The coach said humbly, "The game was won by a freakish play that was very questionable. I think you boys were in the best condition and deserved to win." Then, quietly he turned and walked through the door and on out of sight.*
>
> *Suddenly, I walked up to Weyman Sellers and said: "Coach, I let you down tonight, but I promise you that next year we will beat Rockmart and win the State."*

Now, of course, when I made that promise to Coach Sellers, I had no idea that anything like that could happen. I had no way of knowing. I didn't even know if we'd ever meet Rockmart again, or if we'd have this good a football team again. I was young and impressionable and considered this defeat entirely my fault and without excuse.

We met Rockmart again the following year . . . and I'll tell you that surprising story when I get into my junior year at Athens and talk about the finest football team I have ever played with in my entire life, including college and professional ball.

The two basketball teams I enjoyed playing on the most in Athens High School were in my freshmen and senior years, but we had our *best* basketball teams in my sophomore year. Dallas was playing with me again, of course, and we won the Regional Championship, but lost in the State Championship play-offs to Cairo.

We had another good season in baseball, winning our 4-A Regional Championship, and I pitched two no-hitters.

But football was the big story in my sophomore year, and that loss to Rockmart continued to haunt me.

6

The Busier the Better

There's an old adage I heard somewhere that goes something like this: "If you want something done, give it to a busy person."

During my four years at Athens High School, I took my studies very seriously and was fortunate in maintaining a high academic average. I served as an officer of my classes, and I guess I have been asked a thousand times how I found the time for these things while being a four-letter man (I'd added tennis to my football, basketball and baseball schedule) and devoting myself so constantly to sports.

I don't really know the answer to that, except that I knew by this time the importance of good grades—especially if I wanted a scholarship to college—and I simply *made* the time whenever it was available.

We had a one-hour study hall period each day, and that's where most of the studying was done. Evenings were pretty well taken up with Hi-Y on Monday nights, Junior Civitan on Tuesday nights, and DeMolay on Wednesday nights. In the winter, we played basketball on Tuesday and Thursday nights, and during football season we often had Friday night games. Afternoons throughout the entire school year were devoted to either football, basketball or baseball practice.

So, the only free time I really had was during study

31

period or on weekends, and many's the weekend I would catch up on some lessons.

One thing that helped me was that I loved to be busy and active. Even today I'm involved in several corporations during the off-season and I work 12 to 14 hours a day, loving every minute of it. It's the only way I know how to live, and I wouldn't be happy taking it easy.

Also, I like to read, and the thought of going to study hall, or spending a few hours on a weekend huddled in my books, didn't discourage me a bit. I think most athletes would prefer to be out on the field than to be reading a book, and that was true with me. But, unlike many atheles, I didn't resent having to spend time on studies that I knew would help me tremendously. I found time for both—for the sports I loved and for the studying I needed—and I was determined to stick to it and win in whatever I had to do.

I had a wholesome and exciting social life in high school. I don't think that being a Christian means a boy can't attend parties or have dates or have a good time. He doesn't have to stop smiling. He must abide by certain basic rules, of course, but in so doing he can enjoy himself even more thoroughly, knowing that God is a part of him and that normal youthful fun is in no way trespassing against His will.

Needless to say, I didn't drink or smoke, and I wouldn't consciously join in activities which I thought were wrong. This didn't mean I was a "goody-goody," but God was always very real to me and I don't think anyone could have persuaded me to deliberately go against His will in a serious matter. I stumbled many times, and I continue to stumble, but I always made an effort to live by the rules and ethics which I knew in my heart were correct. I don't want to sound immodest, but I know that any popularity I might have had in high school stemmed as much from my devotion to honesty and fair play as it did from my activity on the sports fields. Even the greatest sports champion has trouble making friends and winning the respect of others if he lets himself go and doesn't have any character and sincerity to back him up.

During my first year with the Minnesota Vikings, I contributed an article to a book entitled *The Goal and the Glory*. This was a book in which some members of the Fellowship of Christian Athletes wrote about their faith. My article was called "Complete Dedication" and I talked about my experiences at the FCA meeting in Estes Park, and about other events which showed my complete dependence upon Jesus Christ, and my complete dedication to Him.

This ability to dedicate yourself to a person or a project is very important, and especially so for the athlete. No boy reading this book doubts that, if he wants to be a professional athlete, he will have to concentrate on his sport right from the beginning and give up many things to attain his goal. It's the same with keeping up a high average in your school marks. These are the worthwhile goals, and the good part about dedicating yourself to them is that the only things you give up are probably not very good for you anyway.

So, if you're wondering how I managed to maintain my marks and be a four-letter man at the same time, the real answer is found in one word: *dedication*. I had a fair amount of brains and good natural abilities in athletics. But none of this would have amounted to a hill of cashew nuts if I hadn't dedicated myself to the development of my God-given talents. There are probably a lot of readers of this book who are starting right now where I started back in my freshman year in high school, and in front of you are a million choices . . . some of them good, some of them questionable, and some of them downright harmful.

But two of those choices can be very simple. *First,* you're in school to get an education. Do your best to get it . . . not only just as much as you need to pass, but as much as you can absorb. *Second,* if you're going out for a sport, concentrate on it and make up your mind you're going to be as good in that sport as humanly possible. In both cases, dedicate yourself to the problem and have a will to win and see it through, being willing to sacrifice yourself for the team or the job at hand.

I hope this doesn't sound like I'm preaching . . . it's just the answer to a question I've been asked by almost everyone who's interviewed me.

And it's really not the complete answer.

I'd struggled with my concept of God during my high school years, as I've already mentioned. My deep faith and beliefs were there, however, and I was always aware of them. I remember an excursion I took in my sophomore year to St. Simon's Island where I visited an historic Methodist Chapel.

I wrote about this trip in my "Li'l Book," and I thank God for the beauty of that chapel, and for the inspiration it gave me . . . and I carried this awareness of God with me when I went on to the football field or faced serious studying. The confidence I had in winning over any obstacle that faced me was solidly based on my faith in Jesus Christ . . . and without it, my dedication to sports and studies would have been worthless.

Where I fell down so badly was in understanding the love of Christ, and there were still two more years ahead before this new dimension to my faith was to take shape and be fruitful.

7

A Promise Kept

When football season got under way in my junior year at Athens, we faced some serious problems. The team had lost seven of its starters, including some of the big linemen, and the general opinion was that we weren't going to have a very good year.

As it turned out, this team was to be called by many the greatest high school football team ever assembled in the state of Georgia. Not only did we have a perfect, no-loss season, but we took our Regional title, the North Georgia title, and the state title. (This was the first time a North Georgia team had accomplished this in ten years, and we took it from Valdosta, a team so powerful it had held the state title for five of the last seven years. Five years later, Valdosta was acclaimed as having the finest high school team in the nation.)

The first thing we had going for us on the Athens team was great speed. We didn't have a man on our starting team that weighed over 190 pounds. And we didn't have a man on our starting team that weighed under 175 pounds. Ed Hanson, our offensive tackle, was second in the state in the 100-yard dash at 10.1 seconds . . . a really tough, rugged 190-pounder. And we had the finest halfback I've ever seen in football —anywhere. His name was George Guisler, and he was my best friend.

George's father was a preacher in a local church

and the family had moved to Athens three years earlier, enrolling George in the ninth grade. He was now a senior and one grade ahead of me.

George was a good athlete and a very fine basketball player . . . but he'd never played football. He actually didn't join our team until later in the season, playing only six games for us, *but he gained something like 1,000 yards in those six games!*

He was one of the most unbelievable performers I have ever seen, and when he went out on a football field he simply and plainly owned it, averaging close to 200 yards in every game he played with us! I have to repeat it, he was just *unbelievable!*

After he'd played about three games for us, this guy who had never played football before received football scholarship offers from just about every major college in the country. And I mean they really wanted him. He finally chose the University of Georgia and I roomed with him when I got there a year later.

Our team went through the season with a 10-0 record and one of the key games was against Richmond Academy from Augusta, Georgia. Richmond was a classification higher than we were and we expected a tough tussle. It didn't help any that I had suffered a shoulder separation earlier in the season and had hurt it again just a week before the Richmond game. The farthest I could throw a ball was about ten yards.

This was also the first game in which George Guisler was playing for us, and if I had had any idea of what he was like on a football field, I would have stopped worrying right then and there.

During the first half, Guisler had been playing at end and fullback and we were losing, 7-0. Our regular halfback hurt his ankle near the end of the half, so when we reported back on the field at half time, my buddy George was the halfback.

"Know the halfback plays?" I asked him.

"Well, I know three of them," he said, studying a

piece of grass as if he were relaxing on a picnic.

"*How* many?"

"One, two, three."

"Good grief!" I said. "What are they?"

"Well," said George, seeing my concern and trying to be fatherly, "I know that little five-yard flutter-pass play of yours. And I know two running plays. One is the regular old-fashioned dive play off the Split T series, just the plain hand-off; and the other is that fancy fake play of yours where you fake to me, then give it to Billy Slaughter—or fake to me, fake to Billy, then you roll back and pass to me." Having said his piece, he looked up at a pretty cloud formation, absorbed in its feathery beauty. I didn't have any confidence in anything at that point.

"Okay, George," I said pessimistically, "let's give it a try, anyway. We'll try the flutter pass first."

"Good," said George. "Er . . . where do I stand?"

That was the kind of conversation we had before every play, but do you know that we used only those three plays for the entire second half, scoring two touchdowns, never having to punt, and winning the game by a score of 14-7! And this was against a tough competitor, which shows the kind of great team we had that junior year.

As the season wore on (and Guisler learned a couple more plays), we began to beat other teams by gigantic margins. As a matter of fact, we scored over 50 points three times that season. When Guisler wasn't running all over the field like a colt in a pasture, he was busy reading his fan mail from the scholarship departments of about forty universities.

We rolled on in high style, stomping College Park 39-0 for the Regional title and then headed for the play-offs for the North Georgia Championship. Guess who we played.

Right. It was Rockmart! The team I had promised Coach Sellers we would beat.

And beat them we did . . . 26-7!

George knew how much the game meant to me, so

he obliged in his usual casual manner by turning in three touchdowns. Everytime we got in a huddle, he'd say, "Why don't you give me the ball, Fran? I think I'll make a touchdown."

I don't have to say it . . . I was the happiest guy in the state of Georgia that night after the Rockmart game. Even Weyman Sellers broke into one of his rare grins and there wasn't a man on our team who didn't know in his bones that we were going to face the mightiest team in the state for the state Championship—Valdosta High School—and take that title home to Athens! If you remember, that was the second part of my promise to Coach Sellers . . . "we'll win the State."

We played Valdosta on a cold December night in Sanford Stadium. On the opening kickoff, I ran the ball back 92 yards for what I thought was a touchdown, but the referee called a clipping foul and so, of course, no score was made. It was a crazy moment, and for a few wild seconds there I thought we were going to just run away with the whole game. A 92-yard run seemed only natural to us after the tremendous victories we'd been having up and down Georgia.

But we settled down to some real football, and behind the rushing power and receiving prowess of Guisler and Billy Slaughter, we wrapped up a beautiful 41-20 victory.

The Athens fans went wild, but I was quiet and inwardly thankful that I had fulfilled my promise to Sellers. He and I walked off the field side by side, and he knew that every pass I'd thrown that year, every play I'd called, and every thought I had about football, and about leading my team, had been dedicated that year to keeping that two-fold promise I had made a year earlier.

In its classification, that football team in my junior year was awesome in its power. And today, many

years later, the names and events of that year file by
in my mind like spectres . . . Guisler, Slaughter,
Bobby Towns, Carlton James, Chester Leathers . . .
Richmond Academy, Rockmart . . . Valdosta.

8

Change of Plans

I had equal ability in all sports when I was in high school, but I sincerely felt that I was headed for a career in professional baseball.

Football, of course, wasn't as big in those days as baseball, and, in my mind, baseball was *the* sport. More important was the fact that I really loved the game and had done well in it as a pitcher and short-stop. I think I received as much publicity from my baseball activities as I did on the gridiron, and, during my junior year, I even had some contact from a professional scout. To top it off, Billy Henderson, the baseball coach, felt I had a great future in baseball, and when we'd talk over the no-hitters I'd pitched, and see our team play for regional titles year after year, it seemed to add up that baseball was a "nat-ural" for me.

In my junior year, however, an incident occurred that wiped out all the thoughts I had about profes-sional baseball. I continued to play baseball in high school and college, but never again was I going to think seriously about baseball as a profession.

In the middle of the baseball season in my junior year, I was pitching against the Covington, Georgia, team. The batter's name was Willie Moore, a terrific player, and being the competitor that I was, I really wanted to put something extra on the ball to get this guy out.

My best pitch was a fast ball, and I wound up and put everything I had into a sizzling pitch . . . and I felt the tendon snap below my right elbow. It hurt a great deal, of course, and I was relieved on the mound immediately, but I honestly don't think I realized the extent of the damage or how it would impair my pitching. Actually, that pitch to Willie Moore marked the end of my ever being able to throw a baseball properly again.

After that episode, I'd go out for practice and try to lob a few across the plate, but my control and speed were gone. I tried all sorts of heat treatments and other therapy, but nothing helped.

I didn't pitch any more in my junior year, of course, but I hoped my arm would "come back" in my senior year. The year's rest didn't make any difference—as soon as I tried to pitch in my senior year, it was obvious that I was finished as a pitcher with a big league potential. The same was true for other positions. I couldn't make the deep throw from shortstop anymore, and they tried to play me at second, but I couldn't make the pivot to make the hard throw from second base.

Serious as my injury was, I was still able to contribute to the baseball team in high school and college, and, much more important, *it never affected my ability to throw a football*. I'd never feel any pain from that part of my arm when I threw a football, but the moment I tried to throw a baseball with any strength, the pain would come back immediately and affect the pitch.

Realizing a baseball career was over was very disappointing to me, but, as I look back on it, that snapped tendon may have been a blessing in disguise. It's possible I may not have had the exceptional ability it takes to be a professional baseball player, and I also think that no matter how much ability a player has, it's more difficult to "make it" in baseball than in football. It's a bigger game than football, with tremendous numbers of young men training and waiting for a crack at the few openings that come along. I would have enjoyed the competition, but, in retrospect, I'm really convinced that getting baseball off my mind once and for all was a blessing.

For one thing, it really enabled me to concentrate fully on football. As I mentioned earlier, I knew that basketball would never be my game; I wasn't tall enough or fast enough. And now that baseball was out of the picture, I really threw myself into football with complete determination to make it my career.

Over the years, I've seen many athletes, with promising careers, defeated by themselves. In the case of my injury, I was fortunate, because my interest in football was almost as strong as my interest in baseball, and I could turn around and dedicate myself to football with hardly a pause. But what if baseball had been the only sport I wanted? What then? Would that injury have defeated me? Or would I defeat myself by simply giving up?

Many times, I've thought about this question . . . "What if baseball had been my only sport?"

And the answer would probably have been for me to learn to pitch with my *left* arm, or to select another position on the team, with less throwing duties, and work night and day at it until I mastered it.

I know enough about myself to say that I would not have stopped dreaming of a baseball career, but would have done anything to adapt to a new position or a new technique. "Quitting" is one word nobody should recognize.

In all sorts of sports, many of today's champions are men who had grave physical problems in their youth. A scrawny kid becomes a champion boxer . . . a polio victim becomes a champion miler . . . a boy afraid of heights becomes a champion glider pilot . . . again and again this pattern is repeated by men who refuse to quit and don't like to lose.

And I'll pass on a secret . . . a man with only normal abilities, but with a tremendous desire to win, is a tougher competitor than a man with better abilities and less desire to win.

And it holds true for everything we do in life. The champions in every field are those who know how to accept adversity—not with a grin—but with grim determination to be victorious the next time. When a man feels like that, nobody can keep him down.

Reporting to my first football practice in my senior year was a dreary day. I was the only starter left. As a matter of fact, not only did we lose ten starters, including the great George Guisler, but graduation had actually claimed twelve of our first thirteen players (six of them had received football scholarships). I really felt lonely out there on the field, and I knew we were going to have a rough year.

Coach Sellers knew it, too, and, in my judgment, he did his best coaching job that year, making us work out three or four hours at a stretch to get the very best from us. To make things seem darker, not only had we lost most of our good players, but the Athens High School football team had moved up to a higher classification—meaning we had an even tougher list of schools to face. A 4-6 win-loss ratio might not seem very good, but that's what we managed to accomplish in my senior year, and when you consider what we had to work with, I think it was a miracle. Sellers is the inventor of the never-say-die spirit, and it shows in his ability to get the most out of every football team he fields.

One of the funniest—or craziest—football games I ever played was in my senior year against Baylor Prep.

Baylor is a perennial powerhouse, and feeds football players to colleges all over the country. If this had been my junior year, we would have been evenly matched with Baylor, but this year we were tremendous underdogs.

On that particular night, I threw five touchdown

passes . . . which sounds great, but four of them were to Baylor and only one of them was to my team!

We'd made it a policy in this game to stay in the air as much as possible, so that our little freshman and sophomore halfbacks, some of them weighing only 145 pounds, wouldn't get killed. I threw 51 passes in this game, and I guess about 20 of them were caught, and we never punted on fourth down, preferring, in this case, to put up some sort of running offense for the experience.

We lost the game by a tremendous margin—something like 61-13. My passes had been caught, all right, but they hadn't been caught by *my* team! It was an ironic situation that I didn't enjoy.

Any loss is unacceptable as far as I'm concerned, but this game was so unusual, and so comical in many ways, that I don't believe it upset me as much as other losses. We'd made a good try against an infinitely superior team and I remember going home, unhappy, but chuckling to myself all the way. Those 51 passes in the Baylor Prep game still stand as a record for me.

Another long-to-be-remembered game for me in my senior year was in basketball, but it wasn't as humorous to me as that football game.

Our team had gone into the finals for the Regional Championship, and we were in the last minute of play against Decatur, the team that was to go on and win the State Championship that year.

We'd beaten Decatur earlier in the season, and they'd had a win over us . . . so it was a hotly contested ball game right from the start. (I was to find out a couple of years later that my wife, Elaine, was a Decatur student and was in the audience that night.)

I was captain of our team, and when we stole the ball from Decatur with 45 seconds left on the clock, I called time-out so we could compose ourselves and not do anything rash that would endanger our slim 2-point lead.

As fate would have it, the referee had not alerted

me to the fact that our team had already used up its time-outs, so he called a technical foul, which allowed a free foul shot to Decatur. Decatur made the point, putting them only one point behind us, and they got to take the ball out. The ball was thrown in to a very fine Decatur forward, Don Keiser, who was later a great basketball star for the University of Georgia. Don hit a jump shot from about the top of the circle and it went in, giving them a one-point lead and a win in the game.

This loss was a big disappointment to me, and it didn't make me feel any better to know that it was my error that caused it.

Unfortunately, this was my last year in high school and I couldn't make any vows to come back next year and win over Decatur, as I had with Rockmart.

9

Unexpected Help

Football scholarships aren't given out just on the basis of a boy's sports record, and I was mighty glad I had kept my marks at an average of 90. Scholarship offers came in from about forty universities and trying to select the one I wanted to attend was one of the most difficult decisions I've ever had to make.

I visited some of these universities, and I remember those days as being filled with telegrams, telephone calls, letters, chartered plane flights . . . heady stuff for a 16-year-old boy. I wanted to wait until spring to make my decision, but most of the universities wanted a commitment in early December. By December 12, I had somehow managed to narrow my selection down to three universities, but I really had no idea which one I'd finally choose. As a matter of fact, the University of Georgia was third on my list, and for some pretty strong reasons.

In the first place, I'd heard a great deal about how tough Wally Butts—the head football coach at Georgia —could be on his men, and that the whole situation at Georgia could prove difficult. Furthermore, Georgia had two very fine freshman quarterbacks named Charlie Britt and Tommy Lewis. Both of them had been high school All-State Quarterbacks and they were having a good year at Georgia. They had three more years to go, and people told me that if I wanted to be a quarterback in college ball, I'd better forget about the University of Georgia.

Well, there's always a little daring in me when people say things like that, and I considered it a challenge. I wanted to prove that I could go anywhere, against any competition, and play football. So, this aspect of it intrigued me.

However, it wasn't a good enough reason for selecting the college I'd attend for the next four years, and Georgia still remained third on my list. The way I chose Georgia came about in another way.

One Sunday afternoon, as I was pacing the floor and feeling the pressure build up for a decision, my Dad asked me a simple question. "Son," he asked, "have you prayed about this?"

"No, sir," I told him, "I haven't."

And, with that, I went into my room and prayed. I didn't expect God to make the choice for me, but I wanted Him to know that I was willing to make the choice through Him . . . with his help. I needed His help and I was willing to accept His direction.

No great voice came out of the air and told me to go to Georgia. But the instant I finished praying that day, I stood up and knew without question that the University of Georgia was the only school I'd attend. I was confident that this is what God wanted me to do, and nobody was more surprised than I was, because Georgia was still down there on the bottom of my list.

I spent a good part of that summer after high school graduation working on Julius Bishop's cattle and chicken farm to tone up my muscles for college football in the fall. I'd leave home at 5 o'clock in the morning and I wouldn't get back until between 7 and 9 o'clock at night. "Dog-tired" is a word a lot of people use to express fatigue. Well, I really know what "dog-tired" means!

One of the big side benefits of signing with the University of Georgia—something I hadn't thought about too much—was the fact that I could live at home during the off-season. During the fall, of course, I would stay in the dormitory, but when football season was over, I was very glad to be able to go on home to my own room and family and continue living in the old familiar way.

Sportswriters on the local newspapers ssemed happy that I had chosen the University of Georgia. Dad still has some press clippings which express the feelings of these writers that I was a local boy and belonged in a local university. I guess they earned that right when you consider the thousands of words they'd invested in me during the past four years. They didn't want to lose track of me!

One of the funnier things that happened when I signed with Georgia was that Wally Butts tried to sign up Wendell, my nine-year-old brother!

"Gee," said Wendell. "I guess I'd better sleep on it a while!"

My older brother, Dallas, was already a sophomore at Georgia, and though he was expected to make the varsity track team, he had not pursued sports in college. I, of course, intended to do just the opposite, and I even intended to major in physical education so that I could eventually be an athletic coach in college or high school. The more I thought about this, however, the more I realized I needed to get something a great deal more out of my four years in college. I felt that my involvement in football and other sports would be enough to prepare me for a future coaching profession, so I elected to take business administration courses.

In all of these decisions, I was more conscious of God than I had been before, and I'm positive His guidance and help were not far from me in those crucial pre-college months. It gave me a poise and an assurance that were to be essential in the days to come.

Fran Tarkenton's
TIPS ON
QUARTERBACKING

BALL HANDLING *Hands-offs* Operate with elbows in close to sides and not flying out. Always keep ball at **waist level**, and always hold ball with **both hands.** Lay the ball into stomach of ball carrier. Don't slam it into his stomach. Practice handing the ball to running back and securely locking the ball into his stomach. During the hand-off, keep knees flexed. Always be on balance.

BALL HANDLING *Taking Snap From Center* Head and eyes: move head and eyes constantly, from left to right, looking over the field. Once you start the signals, or cadence, fix head and eyes to look straight downfield. Hands: place **back** of right hand firmly against seat of center. Then position left hand **face up** with only left and right palms touching. Knees: keep knees comfortably (slightly) flexed with weight on front part of feet, not on toes. Never stand stiff-legged. Feet: feet should be no wider apart than width of shoulders.

BALL HANDLING *Passing Grip* Use the seam of football for grip. Spread fingers across seams in a comfortable way. (I hook my little finger across fifth cross-seam of laces, but do what is most comfortable for you.) Wrap thumb around ball in good grip, but don't squeeze. A firm and comfortable grip takes practice, especially if you have small hands, but you'll never feel in control of the ball until you've developed your grip correctly. It's worth all the practice you give it. Make the ball an extension of your arm, a part of you.

BALL HANDLING *Passing, correct position of feet and ball* Ball: with good grip, use left hand to help push and hold ball over shoulder at height of head or slightly higher. (Remember, you have **two** hands. The more you can use them together, the more control you'll have over the ball and the less likely you'll fumble.) Don't extend arm completely on the backswing. Feet: no wider apart than width of shoulders. Weight evenly distributed.

BALL HANDLING *Passing; release of ball* The ball should be released from a comfortable position, either overhand or three-quarters back, but never from sidearm position. The wrist gives zip to the ball and should be utilized. Twist your wrist hard to the left as you release the ball. Arm, hand and body should follow through, straight toward target. When throwing, step with left foot in direction of target.

BALL HANDLING *Passing; dropback* Upon receiving snap, turn body and hips to run to a point seven yards behind scrimmage line, but keep eyes focused downfield. You'll be looking over left shoulder as you run back.

LEADERSHIP   The quarterback is a coach on the field. He **must** be a leader and command respect from teammates. He should know every player's responsibility on every play, and he must give credit to teammates when it is deserved. As a leader, the quarterback's actions, on and off the field, will determine how much respect he is shown by teammates. Always remember this, because if you want a winning ball team, you've **got** to have the full confidence of your teammates.

KNOWLEDGE   A quarterback must be a student of football. To know how to call plays, he must learn about defenses. He must learn the reasons for certain defenses and their strengths and weaknesses. His teammates will expect him to know what to do in every situation, and situations can change a hundred times in a hard-fought ball game; so, **know and study your football!**

PLAY CALLING   To be a good play caller, a quarterback must know the strong and weak points of both his team and the opponent's. Never call a play just because it's the first thing that comes to mind. Have a specific reason for calling it that is based upon the immediate need and situation. If you're going to take a risk, such as throwing on third-and-two, figure out beforehand the pass with the best chance of succeeding **for a long gain**. When taking a risk, don't go for two yards: go for a touchdown or long gain.

ROLL-OUT   Speed and quickness are essential. In taking the snap, you should reverse pivot and run to a depth of seven or eight yards. Full depth should be obtained by the time you reach the original position of the offensive tackle. When this position is obtained, you should **stop** if the defensive end has you boxed in, and you should look for a way to pass. If you can get around the end, you should continue working to the line of scrimmage and then decide, as opportunity occurs, whether to throw or run.

HOW TO COMBAT RUSH When a quarterback is getting a hard rush, he's got three weapons with which to beat it: (1) he can throw a short, quick pass before the rush is on him; (2) he can switch to a running game, because a lineman rushing in hard is vulnerable to a run and other quick moves by the quarterback; (3) he can scramble away from rush to gain more time.

HOW TO LEAD RECEIVER I don't advocate throwing to a spot, but to the man with the proper lead. You have to know the speed of your end man and the gait he uses in running patterns. Always throw the ball in front of him, because a pass behind the receiver will most likely be intercepted. Speed of the thrown ball is also an important factor in leading a receiver. The slower you throw the ball, the more lead you must allow, and vice versa.

HUDDLE The quarterback is the only one who should talk in the huddle. If a teammate has a play suggestion, he should tell it to the quarterback between plays. You only have twenty-five seconds to get a play called in the huddle and get the ball snapped to start play. You can't waste time and there can't be any confusion. Keep control of the huddle!

SALESMANSHIP When a quarterback steps into the huddle, he should already have a play in mind, **and he should call it in a positive way without stammering or hesitating.** You're a salesman in the huddle, and you've got to convince the team there isn't any doubt in your mind that the play you're calling will work and is the best.

10

Past Glories Don't Count

The laurels I'd won in high school didn't mean a thing in college. All the fellows on football scholarships were high school stars, and, instead of being at the top of a career, as I was in my senior year in high school, I was now at the bottom of a new career. As I walked onto the Georgia campus for the first time, I promised myself that I would follow the same route I had in high school. I would play hard and work hard, dedicating myself to sports and studies, and not allow myself to slump off in any way. I knew it was going to be more difficult to discipline myself in college, because there would be many new interests and college life would be much more demanding than high school. But I was here to get a good education and to further my sports career. These were truths I did not forget during my four years at Georgia, and with this attitude firmly fixed in my mind, and thankful for the scholarship and opportunities that had been given me, I set out to win the goals that Georgia offered me—a ticket into professional football and a sound education that would equip me for business.

Quinton Lumpkin was the coach of our freshman team. Of great importance to me was the knowledge that I could play college football, and even though I had done well in high school, there was always a doubt that I could really make it in college. Coach Lumpkin was aware that many college freshmen feel this way, so the very first thing he did was to restore the confidence of his freshman players by talking to them and encouraging them. Coach Lumpkin meant a great deal to us on the freshman squad, and he won tremendous respect and love from every player. His confidence and optimism were just what we all needed and it wasn't long before he had shaped us into not only a good team, but a really outstanding one . . . some say the best freshman team the University of Georgia ever had. I wouldn't know about that, but, in the three games we played, we were undefeated and, for the first time in ten years, we won the game with our perennial rival, Georgia Tech.

I was captain of the team in this game with Tech, and I remember that my Dad served as Chaplain. In a pre-game mealtime talk. Dad held up a yellow-jacket he'd caught and said, "Fellows, I got me a yellowjacket today. Now, if each of you will go out there today and get a Yellowjacket (the team name for the Tech freshman squad), we'll go home the winners."

It relieved the tension considerably . . . giving us the good spirits we had to have to capture a win in this classic football contest, probably the most publicized college freshman football game in the country . . . and especially in the South, where University of Georgia vs. Georgia Tech games are considered as exciting as the Army-Navy game is nationally.

Nearly 40,000 people had crowded the stadium for the game, and I held a brief moment of prayer with my teammates before we took the field. I didn't play to win. I prayed that we would do our best and live up to the excellent training and abilities we had.

We won the game, 13-7, climaxing the freshman squad's first undefeated season in nearly twenty years, and it was the first time in ten years Georgia Tech had taken a beating from us. To celebrate, we gave Coach Lumpkin a shower with his clothes on, then posed for pictures amid a general hullabaloo in the dressing room.

Our win over Tech must have lighted a fire under the varsity team, because, a couple of days after Thanksgiving, they defeated Tech for the first time in eight years!

At the end of the season, I was selected as a member of the All-Southeastern Conference Freshman Football Team . . . an honor I'll always treasure, because it was the first recognition I had received as a college player. Coach Lumpkin, and the experience on the freshman team, washed away any doubt that I had three fine football years ahead of me.

During fall football practice—which is all work— our team scrimmaged the varsity team to a standstill on several occasions. One day, we outscored the first string varsity team in a game-type scrimmage. Of course, each of us had his own eye on making the varsity team the next year, and I was hoping for it most of all. Charlie Britt and Tommy Lewis had a good year as alternating quarterbacks on the varsity, —they were really great—and I knew I'd still have to win my post the hard way. But already it was being publicized that Georgia had the three most promising quarterbacks in Dixie, and I don't mind telling you I was glad to hear the sportswriters say *three!*

Another wonderful thing about that great freshman team was the number of really good friends I made . . . friendships that have lasted. Pat Dye, who later became an All-American guard for Georgia, was a very close friend. Ironically, he was a great guard on the Richmond Academy football team that we had beaten in high school during my junior year . . . or, I should say, that George Guisler had beaten. Pat and I were co-captains of the Georgia freshman team and we were also to be co-captains of the varsity team in 1960.

I made many close friendships on this team—Phil and Tommy Ashe, Tommy Paris, Fred Brown, Roy Betsill, Bill Godfrey, Bubba Lawrence—and I especially remember Bobby Walden. He was a kicker and halfback from Cairo, Georgia, and he played with me in 1966 on the Vikings. He was our punter, and he was also my roommate on the road trips.

So, you can see that from every aspect this was a tremendous freshman team, not only in football ability (we were scored on only once, and that was by Georgia Tech), but also in comradeship.

I'd also be remiss if I didn't mention that I met my future wife, Elaine, during my freshman year. I'd joined a fraternity, Sigma Alpha Epsilon (old Sleep and Eat), which I enjoyed very much, and, through the fraternity activities I met Elaine. She was a sorority girl at the University of Georgia, Alpha Delta Pi.

All in all, I'd say that freshman year at the University of Georgia *has* to be one of the most fortunate and rewarding years of my life . . . and certainly the most meaningful experience of my life occurred the following summer when I attended the Fellowship of Christian Athletes Conference in Estes Park.

I had prayed to God concerning my choice of a university . . . and, as you have seen, God quickly answered me in many wonderful ways.

When I returned that summer from the FCA Conference, God had become centered in my life. There was absolutely no doubt in my mind that the abilities and talents God had given me were to be used to glorify His name. I was not certain where God would lead me in the future, but, after the past few years in which my name had begun to rise in football, I suspected my future would be in professional football. There would be notoriety, publicity, fame . . . but it was clear to me that all of these things had to be used for the glory of God. God was telling me to witness for Him, and he was offering me a career that would enable me to win the respect of millions and share my faith with them. I knew all of this just as surely as the fact that the earth is round, and as soon as I returned to the University of Georgia for my sophomore year, I set about establishing an FCA chapter on the campus.

During the next three years, I spoke to many, many church and youth groups. I didn't come to them, saying, "See, you, too, can be a star football player if you believe in Christ." This has never been my message. My message is this: "God is love. He cares. He picks you up and is a constant companion in good times and bad. With Christ in your life, you have a fuller life, a more satisfying life, a more meaningful life—whatever your chosen work may be."

As word spread in my sophomore year that I was speaking to young people, invitations poured in at an alarming rate . . . so many that it was just impossible to answer them all. I had to turn down many invitations and I always did it with genuine regret, feeling that somehow I had let God down. Perhaps this attitude begins to show you how much I had changed since the FCA Conference. More than anything else in this world, I wanted to serve God, share my faith, and witness to Him whenever and wherever I could. It was absolute and total dedication, immeasurably stronger than even my desire to play football—though I knew that football was the key that opened the doors to church and youth groups and enabled me to witness. In God's plan for me, football and witnessing were intertwined, and I saw it clearly.

This conviction that football was the vehicle through which I could glorify God's name was responsible, in part, for my joining the Methodist Church in my senior year. There were deeper reasons, of course, both technical and theological, but the fact that I couldn't even be a member in good standing of my former church if I played football on Sundays—a requirement in professional football—added weight to my decision. By this time, I knew I was headed for a professional career, and I knew I would have greatly expanded opportunities to witness to my faith as more people came to recognize my name. I had seen professional athletes witness at Estes Park, and I was living proof of what their witness meant to a young boy. I couldn't think of giving up this same opportunity to testify to God's love just because I wasn't allowed to play football on Sunday.

Anyway, this was one of the reasons I joined the Methodist Church, and my first minister, Reverend Charles Boleyn, understood my problems and guided me ably and meaningfully. He was particuarly helpful in revealing the true love of Christ to me, apart from a million rules and "don'ts," and, as this was the real motivating force behind my disillusionment with my former church, I grew quickly and steadily in a greater understanding of the love of Christ.

My FCA activities didn't stop, of course, when I joined the Vikings in 1961. I started an FCA chapter in Minneapolis and, if anything, my speaking engagements increased. During my first three years with the Vikings, I would spend an average of three or four nights a week speaking to church and youth groups. Also, I did a great deal of writing for magazines and newspapers, and even contributed to books. In many ways, then, I endeavored to spread my Christian witness as far as possible, desiring success on the football field, not only for the team, but so that more people would hear of me and give me an even greater opportunity to share my faith with them.

This witnessing responsibility is shared by all the members of the FCA, because athletes traditionally have the attentive respect of young people—millions of them. They look up to us and want to emulate us, and the responsibility the athlete faces is awesome. The things we say, and the things we do, can affect the lives of young people we've never seen—and members of the FCA pray unashamedly for God's help and guidance before they speak to youth groups.

For this reason—because of the influence athletes have on young people—I rank the Fellowship of Christian Athletes next to the Christian Church in its power to mold and make a meaningful witness to youth. That is a tremendously strong statement, but

I mean it sincerely. When a big, 270-pound All-NFL tackle gently puts one of his ham hocks on the shoulders of a 140-pound high school student who idolizes him, and then speaks softly about the love and companionship of Christ in his life, that, my friend, is a witness!

And it's not so hard to understand why it comes from an athlete. Athletes deal in hard realities; losses and wins are not hypothetical. And athletes are emotional. The prospects of winning can go up and down several times in a game, creating tremendous spirit in a team and causing individual emotions of every kind. And athletes have to work with their talent, too, because it's not guesswork or ignorance that outthinks and outplays a tough competitor—brains and forethought and instant decisions underlie every move a team makes.

These things—reality, emotion, intellect—the athletes' stock in trade, are at the foundation of Christianity, and the athlete, by his very nature, sees the truth and meaning of Christ more quickly, sometimes, than others. Christ is real—very, very real—and He must be accepted with the heart and the mind, and this is language an athlete can understand.

So, I thank God for the Fellowship of Christian Athletes. Not only is the FCA a powerful force among athletes, but its Christian testimony to the world is indisputably of tremendous meaning, and I urge everyone to keep an eye out for a meeting where an FCA member is speaking. Go to it and listen. It will be an experience you'll never forget.

I know.

11

My Strangest Season

"My Strangest Season" might seem like an odd chapter title, but it's the only one that fits my sophomore football season. Everything that could happen to a football player happened to me . . . and then some. And it all started and ended with Wally Butts, head football coach at the University of Georgia.

Before I begin, I want to state unequivocally that Wally Butts is the greatest football mind that I've ever been associated with, and I've been associated with some of the really great football thinkers in this country. I am totally indebted to this man for sharing some of his genius with me, and although Coach Butts and I had some major disagreements (I'll tell you about a few), I love him like a father. I've never known a man whose abilities I respect more.

When I reported for fall practice in my sophomore year, Charlie Britt was first string quarterback, Tommy Lewis was number two, and there I was, just like people had said I would be before I went to Georgia, playing third string quarterback and looking for all the world like I wouldn't get a chance to really play. About a week before the first game—with Texas—I had actually heard a rumor that I might be "held out" a year. In the Southeastern Conference, this means that I could be held out of competition for a year, but still have three more years of football eligibility remaining. Not only did this mean I might have to go to college for five years—something I didn't want to do—but it also meant that I'd be sitting on the bench for a year, and just the thought of this about killed me. During our unbeaten freshman year, during spring scrimmage, and even over the summer months, there had been steady agitation in the press for me to play first string ball. I had never received a better press, I had never played better football, and now, all of a sudden, it appeared to me that Wally Butts was just going to slap me on a bench and let me warm it for a year. I was bitterly disappointed, and though nothing had been said to me directly by Coach Butts, I was sure in my heart that he'd made up his mind not to let me play. It might have been because he simply didn't like to put sophomores on the first string. I don't know. But, whatever the reason, it was a crushing blow to me.

Whenever I'm disappointed, or have a tough problem to work out with myself, I like to get into my car and drive . . . just drive. I'm emotional, and I like to be by myself. So one afternoon after practice, I got into my car and drove all around the countryside on the outskirts of Athens in Clarke County. I prayed about my problem, and I even cried about it. I don't believe I have ever been quite so upset. Anyway, it helped get things out of my system, and, as is often the case when I've talked with God about a seemingly impossible situation, I came away feeling better and determined to work harder and try harder and fight my way through, no matter what the odds. I didn't know what would happen for the rest of the season, but I knew I could quarterback as well as anyone on the team and that the best thing I could do would be to wait for my opportunity and prove it to Coach Butts.

A week later, we went to Austin to play a fine University of Texas football team. I didn't figure I was going to play in the game if Coach Butts had anything to do with it, but I was counting a litle bit on some kind of miracle happening.

Near the end of the first three quarters, Georgia was behind 7-0 and hadn't picked up even one first down. Texas wasn't exactly tearing our team apart, but they were playing us to a standstill and it was embarrassing. I can't say I was really sitting on the bench all this time, because I was up and down, tugging on the shoulder of Johnny Rauch, our Backfield Coach, pleading with him to put me into the game. Then I'd go over to Coach Butts and do the same thing. I'm certain to this day that neither one of them had any intention of letting me play football that night.

With about a minute to go in the third quarter, Texas punted dead on our five-yard line, giving us 95 yards to go. Just at this moment I had made my way back to Coach Butts, after another unsuccessful attempt to shake Rauch into giving me a chance, and I said to Butts: "Let me go in now! Let me go in now!"

"Okay," said Coach Butts, "go in!"

I paused for a moment, letting the miracle sink in, then, realizing that Coach Butts probably didn't know what he was saying—he probably wasn't even conscious he was talking to me—I flew out across the field, scared to death he'd wake up and recall me.

Well, we started a drive on our five and it didn't end until we were sitting in the Texas end zone. A five-yard pass to Aaron Box gave us the first score of the night, putting us one point behind Texas.

We now had a choice of kicking for a tie, or passing or running for a two-point conversion. I told the fellows we'd go for the two points and a win, which was the reason we were out here. I called a pass play, threw the ball to George Whitton, and we were winning 8-7 with eight minutes left to go in the game.

Now it was Texas' turn. They received the ball and rammed it right down the throat of our defensive team, going ahead 14-8. This left about four minutes more to play and I stood up, ready to go back in as offensive quarterback.

But it was not to be. I stared at Coach Butts incredulously as he motioned Charlie Britt onto the field. Charlie Britt was a fine player, and is still a very good friend of mine, and I don't know that I could have done any better than he did. But I felt I had *earned* the right to get back into that ball game! The team had gone for three quarters without a score or even a first down, and, in a few minutes of play, I'd led one drive that had actually put us ahead of Texas. In my book, this was my ball game and I was really shaken up when coach Butts didn't let me finish what I'd started. I watched in sheer misery— and maybe some anger—as our team went down to a 14-8 defeat.

The next week we played Vanderbilt University, and there had been many write-ups that Tarkenton should be playing. The sportswriters had witnessed the Texas episode and there was really a tremendous amount of pressure from the press to put me in as quarterback. But Wally Butts isn't easily persuaded by sportswriters and he let me go in for exactly three plays, then he pulled me out of the game.

Whatever I might have thought at the time, I know now that Wally Butts didn't have anything against me. He just didn't want sophomores playing varsity ball. In his judgment, for whatever reasons he might have had, he didn't want me in there. He knew what I could do . . . he'd seen it during my freshman year, and he'd seen it in Texas the week before. Of course, nothing he could have said at the time would have made any sense to me at all. But, as I said earlier, and as I learned in the next two years, game by game and play by play, Wally Butts is the best football mind I've ever known—bar none.

And then there was George Guisler. (Remember George from my junior year in high school, the half-back who averaged close to 200 yards in every game he played with us?)

Well, George was on our sophomore team at Georgia, too . . . and I roomed with him. With the fabulous George on the team you might automatically expect that we won every goal post we looked at. But George had changed. He still ran with the same authority, and, once in a while, he'd look like his old self. But his interest in the game had dwindled. He never did become the player in college that he had promised to be in high school. I won't speculate on the reasons, because I don't know the answer. But more than once I looked over at Guisler, wondering by how many extra points we'd win a game if he could capture his old form.

Rounding out this strangest of all football seasons, Coach Butts began to play me more as offensive quarterback and moved Charlie Britt into the defensive quarterback position. It worked out very well, and, when my junior year rolled around, Charlie played defense and I played offense almost exclusively. We were in one-platoon football at the time, which meant we had a wild-car substitution, enabling us to switch quarterbacks as we did, one for offense and one for defense.

We only won four games in my sophomore year, but we beat Tech—our school was never to lose to Tech during my four years there—and this was a big thrill for all of us, especially since we'd not done too well throughout the season.

At the end of the season, I was again selected quarterback on the All-Southeastern Conference Football Team, and I felt that my quarterbacking and field generalship had improved immeasurably under the guidance of Wally Butts.

So, Coach Butts, if you're reading this chapter, thanks for being the finest coach in football.

12

Number Four Team in the Nation

As my junior year got underway, Charlie Britt
and I had been picked by sportswriters as the best
quarterbacks in the Southeastern Conference. Despite
this, and other signs of a strong team this season, the
experts predicted that Georgia would finish tenth in
our twelve-team conference. Personally, every man on
the team knew better, and so did Wally Butts.

We started off the season by beating Alabama 17-
13, the only game Alabama was to lose in the entire
year, and the first time since 1954 that Georgia had
won an opening game. I completed six of seven passes
in this game, five of them caught by Gordon Kelly,
a 6'4", 212-pound senior from Decatur.

Our Bulldogs were named Southeastern Conference Team of the Week after the Alabama win, but
the sports prophets were still predicting a big losing
season for us.

The next Saturday, it was Vanderbilt, where I again
connected for six of seven passes, and we won by a
score of 21-6. I was placed on the Associated Press'
All-American checklist, and so was my good buddy,
Pat Dye. The win against Vanderbilt was another in-
dication of the power our team had that season, but,
in the eyes of many, Georgia was just having a lucky
streak.

The pessimists had some cause to point their fingers at us the next week; we took a drubbing from

South Carolina, 30-14, and we were mighty dejected when we returned to the dressing room. We held a post-game prayer that afternoon and we didn't ask to win the rest of the games on the schedule. We asked only that we conduct ourselves like Christians on and off the field, especially in the face of everyone's lack of confidence in us, and we asked that we might train and play harder in the future. This post-game prayer lifted the spirits of our fellows, and we were determined to prove that we were not the "same old Georgia" team, and that our loss to South Carolina was an upset.

Our next three games were against Hardin-Simmons, Mississippi and Kentucky. Everyone of our boys played his heart out, and we won all three games, taking over the Southeastern Conference lead! This was a tremendous surprise to everybody but us, and there's no need to tell you how our spirits were boosted! Georgia hadn't had a Southeastern Conference Championship since 1948, and we were definitely hot on its track after the Kentucky win. Even the press began to change its tone, and you'd be amazed how the prognosticators began to change their minds on their earlier opinions. Wally Butts and the University of Georgia deserved a title this year, and we had the team to give it to them.

We headed south to Florida State University, and then to the University of Florida, winning both games and giving us a 7-1 record. Only one team now stood between us and the Southeastern Conference Championship—mighty Auburn, and in this key game there were many unforgettable moments.

There was no doubt that the Georgia team had captured the hearts of the South. We were truly a "Cinderella" team, having come up from nowhere and having never been given a chance to win more than a couple of games, let alone take the SEC Championship and go into a Bowl game. So, 55,000 fans packed themselves into Sanford Stadium for our game with Auburn—the game that would decide the championship—and I remember thinking, as our present team poured out onto the field, that it was in my junior year in high school that our team took the state title, and wouldn't it be something if we could take the SEC Championship in my junior year in college!

As the game with Auburn progressed, we found ourselves in a tightening noose. Auburn had a very strong defensive team which included three All-American linemen, Zeke Smith, Ken Rice and Billy Wilson, and with only two minutes left to play in the game, we were down 13-7, and Auburn had the ball.

Suddenly, Pat Dye, our great All-American guard, recovered an Auburn fumble at about the 50-yard line, and our offensive team took the field. Trying everything I knew, we managed to drive the ball down to Auburn's 13-yard line with 30 second remaining on the clock. The pressure was tremendous. I could actually feel it tighten me up, and the crowd was going wild—55,000 screaming, hollering voices and we were only 13 yards away from the SEC Championship; but only 30 seconds left to play and it was fourth down, the moment of truth.

I called time-out, fighting for calmness and a chance to think. And then I did something very unusual; I walked away from the huddle, closed my eyes and asked for God's help. My praying is done before a game, and after, but I almost never pray *during* a game. But this time was different, because I simply didn't know what else to do. We had exactly one final chance to win this game. The next play *had* to be the right one.

When I returned to the huddle, reassurance and confidence had flooded over me. The pressure was gone and I didn't even hear the screaming of the fans. All I can say is that I knew God was with me and that I felt His presence. At that same moment, a play came into my mind that I had never used before. It wasn't in our repertoire, we had never practiced it, and I had to explain it in the huddle.

The new play called for me to take the snap from

center and roll out to the right. I'd asked Bill Herron, my left end, who was in at a tight position, to run down and block the defensive tackle. He was to hold the block for approximately four seconds (counting 1001, 1002, etc. to himself)—and then *break* to the left corner of the end zone.

Now, I was hoping that with my roll-out action to the right, and Herron blocking, the defensive half-backs would run to the side of the field I was on, leaving Herron wide open.

Well, I called the play, rolled out to the right, and, sure enough, the defensive halfbacks ran over to my side of the field. As soon as I though Herron had had time to reach the end zone, I stopped and wheeled and, lo and behold, Herron was so wide open it scared me!

I threw the ball automatically, without even thinking, and I'm glad I did, because I was so astounded I almost choked when I saw Herron standing over there all alone in the end zone. I hit him perfectly at the goal line, Herron stepped over and the score was tied up 13-13!

We elected to kick for the winning point, and our kicker was Durwood Pennington, a fellow with ice water in his veins. Durwood came in, without the slightest sign of nervousness, and calmly kicked the extra point.

I walked over to Durwood and congratulated him on kicking the winning point.

"Not me," he said, looking surprised. "You-all got the winning point on that last touchdown."

"No we didn't," I said. "The score was tied when you came in."

He paused for a moment, a strange expression on his face, and said, "Oh my goodness! I had no idea that was the winning point!"

He looked white as a sheet!

Absolute pandemonium cut loose in the stands and on the field! It must have taken twenty minutes for us to make our way back to the dressing room, and every man on the team was crying and laughing all at the same time. I was doing my share of it, too, but later, when the crowds had gone and the noise had stopped, I went off into a corner by myself and thanked God for His help, and for the confidence and poise He had given me in one of the most crucial moments I've ever had in football.

Many times, in talks before youth groups, and in articles and books, I've told this warm, simple story. I don't believe God "takes sides" in football games. But I believe He enables those who trust Him to do their best.

The next week, we played our perennial rival, Georgia Tech, and although it was almost anti-climactic, we wanted this win as badly as we did in any other year. We rounded up 21 points in the first half, then stood on this lead to win the game 21-14.

We accepted the Orange Bowl bid and met up with the tough, cagey Missouri Tigers. I threw a 29-yard pass to Bill McKenney in the first quarter, which gave us our first touchdown, and then, in the third quarter, I hit Aaron Box with a 33-yard touchdown pass that sewed up the game for us 14-0. The two passes had done it, and some sportswriter put a new label on me: "The Praying Passer."

Charlie Britt and I won the Most Valuable Player awards for offensive and defensive quarterback, and Wally Butts won a much-deserved United Press International award as SEC Coach of the Year. He's been heard to say that winning the Auburn game was the most thrilling moment he'd ever experienced in football, and I'm happier than anyone else that our team gave that moment to him.

Other awards came my way that year, yet if I had won every award there was to win, but did not have the love of God, or did not know that His presence was with me, everything would have been worthless and hollow, and there would have been no meaningful victory of any kind.

During the spring of my junior year, and during the following summer, I did a great deal of speaking, I knew more than ever that my ability in football was given me by God so that I could honor Him and share my testimony with an increasing number of people. I spoke every chance I got, while, at the same time, I did not neglect my university studies.

Again, as in high school, I had worked diligently to keep my marks at a high level. I attended the Business Administration School and, because I thought I might like insurance, I majored in it in my junior year and did a pretty good job of selling insurance over the summer. I made some money, and the work wasn't difficult, but I really didn't care for it. It just wasn't my cup of tea.

When I went back to school in the fall, for my senior year, I changed my major to General Business. I took courses in economics, business law, marketing, accounting, real estate, statistics, etc., finding them interesting and more suited to my tastes.

Other events were also keeping me pretty busy between my junior and senior years. After my good junior season, I began to receive letters and questionnaires from the teams in the National Football League, feeling out my interest in playing professional football and asking for more detailed facts about me. I really became very excited about the possibilities of playing professional football.

I still had a year to go at Georgia, however, and as captain of the 1960 Bulldogs, I put first things first and concentrated on the season immediately ahead. It promised to be a difficult one, because we had lost many of our good men—especially ends—and every team in the Conference would be out to get us and knock us off our pinnacle.

13

Farewell to Georgia

As difficult as our prospects for the 1960 season might have appeared, especially with the loss of Charlie Britt (which kept me hopping most of the time between defensive and offensive quarterback) remember that this senior team was really composed of the nucleus of our unbeaten freshman team—and I knew what that team could do. As a matter of fact, I felt that our team this year could be better than our SEC Championship team of the previous year. This wasn't just hope and optimism. I really meant it. Georgia hadn't lost to Georgia Tech once since our freshman team took to the field in 1957, and with boys like this we could go anywhere.

A really great loss, however, resulted from the death of J. B. Whitworth, a defensive coach who had come to us in the spring in 1959. "Ears" Whitworth had been a head coach at Alabama for a few years, and, before that, he'd been an assistant coach under Wally Butts during the great years of Georgia football in the middle and late forties. Coach "Whit" had been a great force in solidifying our football team in 1959 and he had been an inspiration to all of us. He died of a heart attack in the winter of 1960, just before spring practice, and we all felt the lack of his warm, personal brand of guidance. In fact, Coach Whitworth was the perfect complement to Butts, and I really believe that if Whitworth hadn't died, he and

Coach Butts might have led us to another SEC Championship.

We lost our opening game with Alabama, but our guys were really catching them that day. I completed 15 of 31 attempts, good for 152 yards.

The next Saturday, we got our wheels under us and beat Vanderbilt, 18-7. This was a hard-fought game in which I spent about as much time on the ground as in the air, and I remember I collapsed in weariness on my bench in the shower room, being convinced this was the most tiring game I'd ever played.

To prove my point—that this year's team could be a better one than last year's team—we waded into South Carolina, the only team that had beaten us the previous year, and won a very satisfying 38-6 victory. South Carolina was just about the same team it had been last year, with 28 returning lettermen.

We lost to Southern California in the Los Angeles Coliseum, but then we came back East and took Mississippi 20-17. After this game, the Associated Press sent out a dispatch crediting me with leading the nation in pass completion percentage (.592) and with being third in passing yardage (672).

After beating Kentucky 17-13, and then clobbering Oklahoma 45-7, we had five wins in seven games played, not quite as good as the previous year when we had a 9-1 season, but we were still a formidable contender for a second SEC Championship. And then I got us into a little bit of trouble. . . .

On the eve of our game with Florida, I suffered a very bad attack of an old ailment that had been with me, off and on, since 1953. The doctors called it an asthmatic condition. It was due to an unknown allergy, and an attack could come upon me suddenly, without warning, and I would literally have to fight for my breath. Just breathing became the most difficult job in the world. A doctor had even told me once that college football would probably not be possible for me.

When it happened this time, just before the Florida game, I didn't want to go to a doctor who might tell me to stay out of the game, so I went to bed, figuring I could fight it off.

I guess I didn't do too good a job at it, because the next morning at breakfast, the team physician, Dr. Hubert, detected my illness and immediately began medication that was kept up until game time. I was a little punchy from the medication, but I managed to muddle through most of the game until one play in which my receivers were covered and I made a run for the goal, collapsing just as I hit pay dirt. I was "out." They had to carry me from the field, but the worst part of it was that a Florida player had run into my hip when I was on the ground, injuring it pretty severely.

Somehow I got back into the game, playing on instinct, and they told me later that I had completed 24 of 28 passes for 148 yards. Florida won the game, 22-14, and even though I knew I wasn't responsible for the asthma attack, I still felt personally responsible for this defeat. It effectively wrecked any remaining chances we had for a shot at the SEC Championship.

In our next game—with Auburn—I was under strict orders not to run with the ball. As I like to be free to move a ball any way I can when a play is blocked, I knew the team would have to make up for my deficiency. My hip was actually so heavily bandaged I couldn't have run if I'd wanted to. Two good replacements, Dale Williams and Jake Saye, were capable of taking over my duties if my performance really slowed down, so I just did the best I could.

A 22-yard kick gave Auburn the win, 9-6, a close decision which shows you the true strength of our team, with half a quarterback, against a formidable competitor.

With my injury well along toward recovery, we faced our archrival, Georgia Tech. This was to be my last game for the University of Georgia, and as I walked out that day to face our most worthy opponent, knowing that this would be the end of it, I had many emotions . . . exuberance for the game, yes, but sadness and melancholy at the thought of leaving the University of Georgia. This was one time I didn't want to see a game end. I just wanted it to continue, I suppose, into some never-never land.

We won the game 7-6. Pat Dye gave us the margin of victory by blocking Tech's try for an extra point. The last play of the game just happened to be my interception of a Tech pass . . . and then, all of a sudden, it was over.

I remember standing there in the middle of the field with the ball in my hands, the crowds pouring out of the stands and onto the gridiron, and I was oblivious of everything. I was crying a little bit.

And I quietly thanked God for having let me play football for the University of Georgia.

I received every award that year a boy could hope for (the publishers have appended statistics), but the biggest event of 1960 was my marriage to Elaine. We were married on December 22, 1960, and we had to postpone the best part of our honeymoon until January because I was scheduled to play as Co-Captain of the South's squad in the Blue-Gray All-Star game on December 31, with practice starting December 24.

I also received an invitation to play in the East-West All-Star game in San Francisco, but this was on the same date as the Blue-Gray game, so I had to make a decision. It wasn't a hard one; Coach Butts was on the coaching staff of the Blue-Gray team and he had asked me to play with his team.

I took Elaine with me to Montgomery, Alabama, where the Blue-Gray game was to be played, and I accepted an invitation to play in the Hula Bowl in Hawaii on January 8. I figured that would be a fine place to complete our honeymoon!

I can remember many football games where it rained and rained, but I never waded through so much mud and rain as I did in that Blue-Gray game in Montgomery! The North planted us six feet under with a 35-7 score, and there was my bride rooting for me from under an umbrella somewhere in the stands. The North simply had a bigger, better and stronger football team than we did, and had a big advantage on the muddy field.

That night, Elaine and I flew to Honolulu and had about a week to call our own before the Hula Bowl game on January 8.

I was on the East Squad in the Hula Bowl game and didn't get in until the second period, but I made up for it during the remainder of the game by clicking for 19 of 33 passes toting up 204 yards. Mike Ditka, now a tight end for the Philadelphia Eagles, caught two of the passes for touchdowns and that gave us our win of 14-7 over the Western All-Stars. I won the Governor's Trophy for being the Most Valuable Back in the game.

That evening, as I looked over the beautiful Hawaiian countryside with Elaine by my side, I knew I was more fortunate than any man had a right to be. I had a constant companion in God, I had Elaine, I had risen a long way in the sport I loved, and everything was wedded into a meaningful witness to Christ.

Ahead of me lay another few months of college and then a new life in professional football . . . a life full of challenge and further opportunity to serve the God who had brought me so far.

I was indeed among the most fortunate of men.

14

AFL or NFL?

A big decision I had to make while I was in Montgomery for the Blue-Gray game was where I wanted to play professional football. Pete Rozelle, Commissioner of the National Football League, had sent me a telegram in which he said that teams in the National Football League had expressed definite interest in me, and there had been many wire and news stories to this effect. The American Football League had shown just as much interest, and I found myself in a tug-of-war with myself as to which league to choose. A decision had to be made quickly, and I actually made it there in Montgomery, signing with the Minnesota Vikings before I went on to Honolulu.

Why did I choose the Vikings? I've been asked that question dozens of times, and there are many answers.

On the minus side, the Vikings were a non-entity in the league. Just formed that year, they had no history. Furthermore, the Boston Patriots of the AFL had already drafted me, offering 40 percent more than the Vikings. That difference was a big one! The Minnesota and Viking scouts had come to Montgomery and I found myself in a tough predicament as to what to do—because despite everything, I really wanted to play in the NFL.

In the first place, the NFL was the more established league, the tougher league, and I knew it would be harder to make it in NFL ball than in the AFL. (It was that old challenge again.) I wanted to prove to myself that I could play with the best and make it. Also, the additional challenge of starting out on the ground floor with a new franchise—an untried team that would need all the talent and ability it could get—interested me tremendously. The thought of being able to help them come up through the ranks of NFL ball to a position of respect and prominence in the league intrigued me greatly.

So, it was the NFL, hands down.

One thing that disappointed me was that I was a third-round choice by Minnesota. I'd always felt that all great quarterbacks were drafted in the first round. (I'd forgotten about Johnny Unitas who, of course, was a free agent, and about Bart Starr who was a *seventeenth*-round draft choice—imagine!) It wasn't until later that Joe Thomas, Minnesota's scout, said that the Vikings were scared they had lost me, but it was essential for them to pick up a running back and a linebacker before a quarterback. When they found me still available on the third round, they grabbed me quickly.

Anyhow, it didn't help my feelings any to be a third choice and it just challenged me even more to go with the Vikings and prove to everyone that I could play with the big boys in the NFL.

I had a lot more to learn, many new things to adjust to, mentally as well as physically, and my first year with the Vikings was filled with many, many surprises.

My first meeting with Norm Van Brocklin was in February of 1961, in Minnesota. Norm had just signed on as Head Coach for the Vikings, and he told me at this meeting that the Vikings had just traded for George Shaw, who had been an alternate regular quarterback with the New York Giants the year before, and was a seven-year veteran of the NFL, and yet only 27 years old. George was to be the starting quarterback and I was to be brought along slowly, going into a game now and then when it was unquestionably won or lost, and generally watching and learning from the bench where I wouldn't be under too much pressure.

This wasn't the kind of talk I appreciated at all, and I couldn't see myself sitting on a bench in professional football anymore than I could in high school and college. I'd faced this problem before, especially in my sophomore year at Georgia, and I knew the only way to change Van Brocklin's mind was to prove myself in training camp and make it crystal clear to everyone that I could play as a rookie, although this is very seldom done in professional football. The next few months in college—even though I was to graduate—went slowly for me because of my impatience to get up to Minnesota in August and start training—and when training began, it started with a bang.

Right off the bat, we had an inter-squad game in Moorhead, Minnesota. George Shaw quarterbacked one team and I quarterbacked the other, and my team won 35-7. I didn't think this would change Van Brocklin's mind about using me as a starter, but I figured it would at least cause him to think about using me more often when the regular season started—not just when I couldn't do any harm, or any good, but when the game was still undecided. I might have been a rookie, but I was determined to make him overlook that as quickly as possible.

In our first exhibition game, with the Dallas Cowboys in Sioux Falls, Norm put me in in the fourth quarter—sticking to his original thesis—and I threw a touchdown pass, the only one the Vikings made in the game.

In the second exhibition game, with the Baltimore Colts, the game I told you about earlier in the book, Norm told me to go in in the second quarter—a big improvement over a fourth-quarter entry—and I accomplished nothing, except to get clobbered by Gino

Marchetti and undergo my true baptism of fire in the NFL. It was a shattering experience and made me realize, reluctantly, that maybe Van Brocklin knew what he was doing.

If I didn't realize it that day, I sure did a few weeks later when we played the Chicago Bears in the fourth exhibition game of the season. In this game with the Bears, I took the worst physical beating of my life. I can't even remember what the score was, or anything about the game, except that when I came back to Minneapolis after the game, Elaine met me at the door and she could hardly recognize me. My legs were swollen, I had cuts on my face, and I looked and felt as if the whole Bear team had used me as the football.

The problem was that I was being introduced to a new, tougher brand of football, and I couldn't get the "feel" of quarterbacking professionally. It wasn't like high school or college ball. This was hard, really hard, and it demanded a whole new outlook. I thought about it every moment of the next week, and I gradually adjusted myself to what I knew I had to do as a quarterback. There were ideas I had to forget, some I had to adjust, and some I had to learn, and when we faced the Los Angeles Rams in the last exhibition game at home, I felt that I had made the adjustment and was eager to get into the game.

Van Brocklin sent me in in the second half. We were behind, 21-0, and I led our team to 17 points. This was not a win, to be sure, but I knew I had begun to successfully make the switch from college ball to professional ball, and I developed the confidence in that game that I needed so sorely. On that afternoon, I started becoming a professional quarterback. It had taken a lot of bruises and some painful experiences to bring it about, but I knew now that I was on my way.

And I think Van Brocklin knew it, too . . . because I was to play much more often during the season than he had originally predicted.

The three greatest thrills in my sports career would have to include the win over Newman High School for the Regional Basketball Championship in my sophomore year at Athens; the great Auburn game in my junior year at Georgia; and, topping them all, the first regular-season professional football game in which I ever played—not so much because it was my first game, but because of how it turned out.

This game was against the Chicago Bears, the team that had administered the beating to me during the exhibition season. A week before this game was scheduled, Van Brocklin had told me I was to be the starting quarterback, but then he changed his mind and said it was only fair to start it with Shaw, the veteran, and the man who had started in the exhibition games. I was disappointed, but I knew Norm was right, and that he'd feel he was only taking a big risk on the first game of the season by starting me so early.

George played the first four or five minutes without much happening, and then Norm put me in with the score 0-0. I admit I was nervous. The Chicago Bears were the oldest team in the National Football League, and one of the toughest, and the Vikings were the youngest. Everything the NFL had to offer in the way of experience and power was opposing me just a few feet away, and here I was, a kid of 21, fresh out of college, being required to lead an untried team into this battle where we'd have to outthink and outfight the old masters.

As part of the buildup to the regular season, I had to memorize approximately 100 passing plays and 100 running plays, and when I came out of a huddle, the opposing team could shift into any of ten or twelve defensive line-ups. These line-ups could cancel the play I'd called in the huddle and necessitate the immediate selection of a new play, a selection that had to be made in a matter of four or five seconds. In facing the Bears that day, I had a "ready list" of plays but I had to fight the temptation to go blank.

And here is where God's strength is so important. It provides an inner peace and calmness.

I have no words to tell you the thrill that swept over me when we won that game 37-13! From the time I was a little boy collecting bubble-gum cards, all I'd ever dreamed about was being a professional athlete. And here was the reality! My first time out and a decisive win over the team with the best overall record in professional football! It was not only a tremendous thrill for me, but it was equally tremendous for the Vikings. Nothing our team was ever to do—even when we tied the Green Bay Packers for second place in the Western Division in 1964—was to surpass the joy I had in those moments of realizing we'd won against the Chicago Bears.

I was the last one to leave the dressing room after this game with the Bears, and I remember walking through the tunnel and out onto the field to recapture the feeling of victory I'd had an hour or so earlier.

The stadium was immense in its loneliness. Where 40,000 noisy people had sat just a little while ago, there was nothing now but scattered papers, torn programs, and empty Coke bottles. The wind whipped up dust spirals on the field. It seemed as if nothing had happened here . . . and I learned something, something important.

The moment of victory is real, but going back is never the same. To make victory live, it must be built upon. I learned I had to take my victories with me and build on them, never looking back. In this way, a victory continues to live and grow. I take the victory of Christ into my life in the same way, and I know I must build on that victory or it, too, will die, at least for me.

A victory that lives only in us, in the heart, mind and faith of man, renewing itself daily in man's life and actions, is the true substance of Christ's sacrifice on the cross and resurrection. This is the true victory, and it leads to a like resurrection for every man who keeps it alive.

Things got worse that year before they got better. I think Van Brocklin started me in nine games and started Shaw in five. I'd been given what I'd asked for, but it was a mixed blessing, because of our poor showing.

After the game with the Chicago Bears, we lost the next seven in a row. We had two victories later in the year in games where I started; we beat the Baltimore Colts and the Los Angeles Rams.

In totaling up the results of that first year with the Vikings, I would say that it was extremely productive for me. Despite the defeats, I threw for 18 touchdown passes during the season, a rookie record.

Most important, of course, was the complete change in my thinking regarding football. Professional football is a game, but it is also a business. A professional football player is being paid to do a job, and if one man doesn't do it, the team's management and coaches will find someone else who can. The pressure, therefore, is terrific, and especially for quarterbacks, because in professional ball a lot of emphasis is put on the excellence of the man at this position. He does the thinking for the team, he pulls the strings that make the team go, and the responsibility for a defeat is almost always placed squarely on the quarterback's shoulders.

During the first season, I'd lose sleep at night and worry about not doing the job I knew I could do. I was a rookie, making rookie mistakes, but I didn't feel I should be making rookie mistakes. I had many such slumps as this, when I'd berate myself for not coming along faster, but by the end of the season, I'd started to straighten out and I was becoming a football player. That first season with the Vikings was tougher on me than my four years in college ball. There's that big a difference between the two.

Actually, I think it takes about four years before a quarterback matures in professional football. And there are many reasons for this.

It takes four or more years before the plays and

decisions under competitive circumstances become second nature to a quarterback. He has to be a coach on the field, he has to know the game inside and out —defenses, offensives, every aspect of the game—and by having this kind of knowledge, he imparts confidence to his teammates: a factor of the greatest importance for a winning football team.

From that four-year period on, a quarterback continues to grow and improve, and is likely to have his best years after age 30. Van Brocklin had his best year when he was 34. Y. A. Tittle hit his heyday when he was 36, 37 and 38. They weren't the same persons physically that they were in their early twenties, but they knew the game inside and out and enjoyed the absolute confidence of their teammates.

I didn't really feel I'd earned my team's complete confidence until I'd been quarterbacking for the Vikings for about four years. But under the tutelage of Van Brocklin, and other good people, my teammates came to know that I could control and run a football game.

This was the hardest part about being a quarterback in my rookie years, because I knew my teammates didn't have confidence in me, and I had to tell crusty old veterans what to do. But thanks to the fine players we had—fine men as well as football players —I never got into too much trouble in the huddles. They usually went along with me, giving me my head, but there was one incident I won't forget.

Hugh McElhenney came back tired to the huddle one time in my rookie year and said, "I'm tired, Fran. Don't run me this time."

Well, here was a direct challenge to my authority in the huddle, and I felt I had to establish in everyone's mind that I was running the game, regardless of whether it was McElhenney I had to buck or anyone else. And, in my mind, McElhenney was, and still is, the greatest running halfback who has ever played football.

Well, king of the halfbacks or not, I gave McElhenney a running play to prove I was a boss of the show. He laughed about it afterwards, and still laughs about it now.

Like I said, that was a fine team.

15

Trials, Triumphs and Scrambling

The Minnesota Vikings had a slow but sure rise in stature over the next few years. Our second year in business was the exception, however, showing only two wins for our efforts (we'd had three wins the first year), but in 1963 we came back and won five football games, a good mark for a young team in the NFL.

Then in the fourth year, 1964, we had great success and tied the Green Bay Packers for first place in the Western Division with an 8-5 record.

I was invited to play in the Pro-Bowl game that year and was co-quarterback with Johnny Unitas, who I still think is the greatest quarterback who ever lived. Getting into the Pro-Bowl game meant a great deal to me, because ever since I'd been in professional ball I'd wanted three things. First of all, I wanted to help win an NFL Championship. Secondly, I wanted to be an All-Pro selection. And thirdly, I wanted to play in the Pro-Bowl game.

I got hot in the Pro-Bowl and led our team to two touchdowns, via passes, and received the Most Valuable Player award. I went to the Pro-Bowl game the following year, also, but didn't repeat my performance of 1964.

One of the most satisfying victories we had in the 1964 season was against the Packers, at that time—as now—one of the strongest teams in the country. We were trailing the Packers by one or two points with two minutes left. It was fourth down, with 22 yards to go on our own 35. Here, again, as in the Georgia vs. Auburn game, I knew we had to have an unusual play to pick up a victory.

I called for a scramble . . . the only time in my professional career I've ever deliberately called it. I told the ends to go down the field thirty yards and find an open spot and I would try to find them. I took the snap, came back to pass, scrambling around to gain time, because I needed plenty of it, spotted Gordie Smith down the field and threw the ball to him. Gordie caught it at the Packer 30 and picked up another five yards before he was tackled. From there we kicked a field goal that won the game for us with about thirty seconds left to play. We'd never beaten the Packers before and this was a great victory for all of us.

Of course, my greatest thrill in professional football is still to come, and that will be when the team I'm playing for wins the championship. If I play football for fifteen years and haven't seen the right side of a championship, I believe I'd come back the sixteenth and seventeenth years, and more, if I thought there was a chance to get it.

One of the things I found out about professional football was that publicity about players was more critical and to the point. In high school and college, the players are amateurs and there is a tendency in the press to take it easy on them, blowing up their winning feats and soft-pedaling their mistakes. It's not like that in pro football, and although I always had a very fair press, I knew that it was generally dependent upon a good performance on the field.

The sportswriters were the first to hang the name "Scrambler" on me, although I was by no means the first person to be so labeled. Frank Ryan, when he was with the Los Angeles Rams, was called a scrambler, but for some reason nobody thought much about the name. Others were called scramblers, too, and in my rookie year some of the writers started applying the term to me. In my case, the name stuck, and by my fourth year with the Vikings the name "Scrambler" had become synonymous with Fran Tarkenton. Especially was this true when we played the Giants in New York in 1964. The New York press had really built up the scrambler image and I guess I helped it along by having one of the most spectacular scrambles of my career against the Giants. I went *thirty yards* behind the line of scrimmage and completed a pass down the field for a ten-yard gain and a first down. This was the only time I scrambled during the whole game. I didn't even get out of the pocket the rest of the day, but there was no doubt that this one scramble was fantastic enough (to me, too) to cement the name to me forever. *Sports Illustrated, Life* magazine, and other newspapers and periodicals picked up the name after that Giants game and it has gained momentum steadily ever since.

I didn't like it when they first applied the name to me. Once or twice in college I'd been called a scrambler, but I thought that it denoted a somewhat freakish quarterback. I really didn't know what the term meant.

When I came to professional football, I brought a philosophy of quarterbacking with me that I thought was a little different from the usual philosophy. I used to watch football on television on Sunday afternoons and I'd see the quarterbacks go back seven yards to pass and if their pattern was there, they'd throw the ball. If they couldn't throw it, they seemed content to take a seven-, eight-, or ten-yard loss without thinking anything about it.

Personally, I just couldn't see it that way. If I didn't have a pattern, or if my pass protection was broken down, I would have tried anything to advance the ball forward. I did a lot of this in college, and, in effect, I was scrambling.

Technically, scrambling starts from a drop-back pass position. It is not a roll-out or bootleg action, as many people think it is. We have roll-out passes in pro football, and we have bootleg passes, but the scramble is not part of it. Once the drop-back pass position has been reached and, for some reason, there's not an immediate opportunity to throw the ball, scrambling begins. Some people don't generally realize this, but I'm a pocket passer. If I throw 25 passes in a game, 21 of them are from the pocket and 4 of them from a scramble situation. Sometimes my pocket will crumble and I have to get out and run. I'll move to the right, or to the left, or down the middle and either throw or run from this position. I always look for a chance to throw before I run, but when my protection folds up, there's no knowing what's going to happen and I depend upon quick feet, quick instincts and good lateral vision to gain a yard or two out of a play that's coming apart.

There have been times when I've been caught in a scramble situation and it's caused us trouble. But a lot of scrambling experience has gone over the dam now, and I can use better judgment about when to scramble and when not to, as well as the particular type of scramble I need to put on, and it's becoming a more and more effective weapon when I use it.

Quarterbacks are more mobile these days than they were, say, a decade ago. The pass rush is much greater than it ever has been before, and scrambling is becoming a virtual necessity for some quarterbacks.

And the philosophy behind scrambling remains the same . . . it's an instinctive effort to advance the ball in any way possible, rather than sitting back there and taking a yardage loss. This philosophy is part of me and it will continue to be. But I only scramble when necessary. I don't make a steady diet of it, and I don't think you can build an offense on scrambling. However, it can get a quarterback out of trouble in emergency situations, and when the quarterback is in trouble, the team is in trouble.

Even after the Giants game in New York, I didn't fully realize how closely I was associated with the

ame "Scrambler" until my last year with the Vikings
n 1966, when I was introduced before a game with
he Dallas Cowboys. We ran onto the field, and as
hey called off the names of the fellows in the starting
ine-up, they introduced me as "The Scramler, Fran
Tarkenton."

I don't mind having a tag put on me, but they don't
have to use it before they use my name!

Perhaps the best way I can sum up my scrambling
activity, and also press home my deepest philosophies about fighting to win, is this way:

I was talking to a writer one time, and he wondered
why I scrambled. He said, "I guess there's no sense
standing back there and getting clobbered."

You know, I had never thought about that aspect
of it, and I quickly corrected him by saying that there
was only one reason to scramble—to win a ball game.
The only thing I think about on a football field is
winning.

It's an important attitude that is just as valuable in
life as it is in football. Let your central thought be:
"How do I advance . . . how do I win . . . how do I
keep going ahead?"

There's no room or time for fear in such an attitude.
And you won't find any time for losing.

16

New Fields to Conquer

Being a professional football player, I was introduced to a whole new way of life, not only on the football field, but also in business. During the off-season with the Vikings, I devoted a lot of time to forming some small companies of my own and I became just as intrigued with business as with sports. They're alike in many ways. Each demands clear thinking. They're equally competitive. Goals are clearly defined. And there are just as many emotional ups and downs in business as there are on the gridiron, requiring a never-say-die spirit and a dedication to winning.

One thing I found out early is that many businessmen don't think a successful business can be built on solid Christian principles. It was one thing, they said, to have faith on a football field, but it's another to practice Christian ethics in business. What they were saying is that I was naive to go into business and expect to abide by my faith.

Well, I'm here to tell you that such an attitude is nonsense. It is so ridiculous and misleading that it became a great challenge to me to correct it. Every business I have today is dedicated to proving to everyone that a man who plays by the rules, and plays hard, as you do in football, has a far *better* chance of success than his competitor who may cheat or take unfair advantage of others.

Not only was it a challenge to me to run my own business this way, but it became imperative for me to express my views to other businessmen. And here again God gave me all the openings I needed, because, as a professional athlete with a good name, I was continually being invited to speak before business and civic groups. Here was a new field that God had set before me. Here was a whole new group of people who respected me and would listen to what I had to say. I knew it would be different, and harder, and that talking to business executives is not the same as talking with young people. But I had successfully made the transition from college to pro ball—which required a 100 percent change in thinking and tactics —and this new challenge didn't faze me a bit.

If you're blessed to have God with you, as a companion and friend, then wherever you go you take God with you. What difference does it make if you're on a football field or in an office? Do you leave God outside just because you change your scenery? And can you put God aside for a few hours while you transact a business deal, and then pick Him up again to accompany you to church on Sunday? Many, many of the businessmen I talked to felt that way. And I ask, what kind of faith is that?

So, I entered into a new field for witnessing, and starting with my second or third year with the Vikings, and continuing until today, most of my speaking is done in front of adult, business audiences. They expect to hear some great football stories, and I give them all they want. But every talk I give has a Christian message. I don't care whether I'm talking to a group of corporation presidents or a convention of young jaycees, my reason for being there is not only for the usual speech, but also to testify to the power of God in my life.

As with football, my desire to win and be successful in business is for the purpose of being able to use the talents God has given me to the fullest in an ethical way. For example, sports-minded young people may be persuaded to consider Christ and God more carefully when they know that whatever I am I owe to God. The same applies to businessmen. If I become a huge success in business, then my testimony to God's help will be food for thought to even the most hardened disciple of unfair business practices.

And if I were to be the most successful businessman in the country, but didn't witness to God, then my success would be meaningless. It's the same way with quarterbacking. If I won every award, and won championship after championship, it would mean nothing if I didn't witness to God.

Now, I'm not the kind of guy who can walk up to a man, take him by the arm and say, "Are you saved, brother?" Other people can do it, and do it successfully. But it isn't my way and I wouldn't be effective in this type of witnessing.

I believe that God gives one opportunities to witness in many different ways, and of course the most effective witness is the way I live my life, and the way I act. If people can't see Christ in me, then I'm lacking something somewhere. But the biggest opportunities come from my speaking engagements, and I never speak to a club or business organization without making it clear somewhere in my talk that I believe in Jesus Christ.

I remember that once I was asked to make a brief business presentation to about 300 outstanding businessmen. Here was a golden opportunity to influence some of the most prominent and wealthy business people in the country. I gave my little talk, and, within it, I included a Christian message. I think the audience was a little stunned at first, but then they applauded, and I know that my testimony did not go unheeded.

I meet a lot of fast, swinging people in the business world, and I've been in many bars and night clubs from New York to San Francisco. Between traveling with the team and accompanying my business associates, there are few places in this country where I haven't set foot. And, if it's a bar, I'll sit down with them and order a Coke. I don't want anyone to think that I believe I'm any better than he is, because I am not. I want my friends to know I care and, hopefully, to learn to know the love of God as I do.

So, the business world has really become a great challenge to me, and I know I've been led into it by God so that I can expand my witnessing activity. It involves new methods of presenting my faith, and I think the following talk which I gave at the Georgia State Jaycee meeting in 1966 demonstrates the typical way in which I approach my new "assignment."

"As sports fans, we are all interested when a major game comes up. Our big question is, 'Who is going to win the game?' We form our opinion. We measure the strong and weak points of the teams, and we make our predictions. But we never really know what the results will be even though we have established our favorite.

"Tonight, I want to project beyond field, court or track and ask another question . . . a question which should really haunt every American. I ask tonight, 'Who is going to win the world?'

"We are living in a world when often the loudest voice shouts down the truest. Often the Klansman . . . the beatnik . . . the racist . . . or the draft card burner projects the image for campus . . . for city . . . for state . . . for region or even for an entire nation. How dangerous it is that so many of us— who really care so much—find ourselves members of the silent mob.

"To whom will tomorrow belong? Will it belong to the racist and the Klansman, the beatnik or the draft card burner?

"I say no!

"We are living in a day when we need a new challenge to courageous living. And we know that to be courageous does not imply that we are without fear. It means that we have been motivated to the point of overcoming fear for a goal. One excellent definition of courageous living is 'to live responsibly with reference to a situation not of our own choosing.'

"The self-servitude of individuals wrapped up only in their own personal desires has never created the inspiration that could go out and win a world. I cannot help but think tonight of Americans who are serving, even at this hour, in Viet Nam. Are they there because they really want to be, or are they there because they 'live responsibly to the ideals of truth?

"There have been many disagreements over the issue of confronting communism on the foreign soil of Viet Nam. None of us can hope to be completely correct, but when the time of personal accounting comes, there is one thing worse than being mistaken and that is being a timid friend to truth.

"I am really wondering who will possess tomorrow's world!

"Each summer, in mid-July, my teammates come from all over America to Bemidji, Minnesota sixty miles south of the Canadian border, away from our families and isolated from the rest of the world. [I was with the Vikings at this time.]

"Here begins a two-month training program that would stagger the imagination of the most enthusiastic physical culturist. Besides technical precision and carefully-planned strategy, there are long and painful hours of running . . . throwing . . . catching . . . knocking and driving to the point of anguish and total exhaustion.

"On a dry day the field is often muddy with sweat and blood. Do we drive ourselves because the coach has said this ritual will guarantee us victory? No! I don't believe that any coach or athlete would be that naive. All the agony, the pain, the

weeks of isolation are endured just for a hope—
the hope of victory!

I am firmly convinced that tomorrow's world
belong to the best competitor. We are a room full
of competitors tonight. These men can be classified
as successful, and every successful man who has
started at the bottom can tell his own story of dark
nights and the long rocky road to success. You
know that winning comes at great cost. Our history tells us the story of competition for lands,
minerals, wealth, fame and power. The whole world
competes. Man's history tells the story of competition from the cave to the moon. But today we
find ourselves on a unque battlefield, for the major
forces of the world are competing for the mind of
man. Psychologically we know that if you possess
a man's heart and soul, you possess him and all
that he owns.

"Because we are Americans, because we go to
church, because we take our children to Sunday
School, because we are members of the PTA, because we belong to a civic or service club . . . does
all this guarantee tomorrow for us? When we talk
about the price or the cost of victory, when we de-
mand sacrifice and discipline, it is well for us remember that we have no sole claim to these char-
acteristics.

"Other ideologies and other philosophies and
other political persuasions exist that in the blink-
ing of an eye would take away from us every
freedom and truth that we hold sacred.

"We must remember that these alien philosophies
are disciplined and dedicated and they are willing
to pay even the price of death for their beliefs.

"Let me tell you my answer to the question.

"The world of tomorrow is going to belong to
the best competitor—not necessarily the best cause.
I know in the world of sports that the best team
does not always win. An athletic team with superior

talent can be defeated by just a little complacency when a lesser qualified, but 'hungrier' team comes along.

"I have complete faith in the righteousness and truth of our way of life. But I am sometimes fearful that a lesser cause will dominate our day because of its competitive drive and our laziness.

"Tonight the Jaycees honor the young men of the year. These men are great competitors who have put dedication, discipline and love to work.

"What makes up a competitive spirit?

"There are several factors: knowledge, drive, ambition, determination, but above all, faith in oneself and in one's cause. A successful competitor must have the faith that allows him to overcome setbacks—to use them as a springboard to his next victory.

"Our forefathers, who won this nation, believing in the freedom of man, had no other goal in mind except to win. I often wonder at a mis-direction of sportsmanship today. I fear that we have given our youth a philosophy of accepting defeat—of being a 'good loser.' There is no virtue in losing. You show me a *good* loser and I will show you a *loser*.

"The young men we honor tonight have exemplified the competitive spirit and have demonstrated the Jaycee ideal.

"The Jaycee purpose reveals that man's greatest treasure lies in human personality and that faith in God gives meaning and purpose to human life.

"The very inception of this organization expresses a strong hope in man. And man's only legacy for tomorrow is what he is willing to put into life today. The impact of his legacy is no greater than his dedication, his discipline and his love. This is not only our defense, but our attack.

"Many, many years ago, when the Greek civilization flowered, the great city-state of Sparta stood alone in the strength of her defenses. A commanding general from a neighboring city-state decided to visit Sparta to see the mighty walls that were said to protect her citizens. When he arrived in Sparta . . . and started looking for the Commander-in-Chief of the great Spartan armies, he walked through legions of strong, sun-tanned young men training in the fields. He was surprised to find no towering walls. Sparta was a city living open to the four winds.

"In amazement he asked the Spartan commander, 'But where are your walls?'

"The Spartan general looked toward the strong young men training on the Grecian fields and said: 'There are the walls of Sparta . . . There . . . Every man a brick.'

"Who will possess tomorrow?

"With bombs, machines, computers, it seems that there has been a de-emphasis of man. I say to-night that our only hope of the future is a re-emphasis of man . . . and a re-emphasis of the faith in God that gives man meaning and purpose.

"Every man a brick!

"I dearly love my little fourteen-month-old girl and only another traveling father can know the agony of being away from one so tender. As I hold her in my arms, as I watch her playfully put her little head in my big dog's mouth, and she is shielded by the security of Elaine's love and mine, I am haunted by the questions: 'Who will direct her thinking, who will guide her future?' In the presence of this assembly . . . and before God . . . I would give my life for the knowledge that the values and the guidelines that have been mine . . . will be hers also.

"Tonight we have talked about materials, men and competition, and we have said that only our faith in God gives meaning to these. Through all our efforts and skills and sacrifices in this material world, still all that we can really have is just the *hope* of victory. But in God's great plan for all men, He has gone a further step . . . and through His Son, Jesus, He has given us the *promise* of victory."

17

Playing to Win

Elaine and I waited four years to have a child, and when little Angie was born in November 25, 1964, I thanked God for an alert, healthy baby.

It didn't concern me that Angie was a girl, rather than a boy, and in many ways, I'm thankful we didn't have a boy, because my tendency might have been to direct him into an athletic career.

I'm older now, and know better, and if we should be fortunate to have a boy in the future, he would never be made to feel that he has to be an athlete. He would make me just as happy and proud if he chose to be a teacher, or a piano player, or a writer, or a doctor, or anything else, provided he dedicated himself to the goals he wanted to achieve and *dared* to give his best to his business or profession.

However, there is one way in which I would lead him—just as I intended to lead Angie—and that is toward acceptance and dependence upon the Lord, Jesus Christ. This is what my life is all about, and although I have not felt the "call" to be a clergyman, I know that I am a minister in the truest sense of the word, and that the pulpit God has given me is far-reaching and very, very important.

I would speak to my son the way I am speaking to you in this book. First of all, I would make it clear to him that I am no Pious Pete. Since I first accepted Christ, I have stumbled and fallen many times. I continue to stumble and fall, and I continue to do things I wish I didn't do. I am not perfect—none of us is—and it is because of this that we need Christ so much. This is the first thing I would want him to know—that neither I, nor he, nor any man is perfect, and as soon as he realizes this he can begin to grow as a person, because he has discovered a basic truth that will lead him to the eventual victory in Jesus Christ.

Then I would want my son to understand that he should not believe in me as though I were infallible. Believing in the perfection of men is the surest way to disappointment and discouragement. I want him to love people, as I love people, but not to the point where he has *faith* in them or worships them. Because sooner or later, the person he has faith in will let him down. Sooner or later, the basic imperfection and fallibility of every man who walks this planet comes to the forefront, and if my son worships a man—any man—he is inevitably due for a bitter disappointment somewhere along the line.

Christ, on the other hand, is constant. Here is One who will never waver. Christ is simply *there* . . . always there, perfect, understanding, helpful, and the source of undying strength and companionship.

When I think of my life, and my Christian faith, one special word always comes to mind. That word is "love." God's love is giving His Son so that we might live . . . God's abiding love for us . . . God's simple request that we accept His love, because there is no way we can earn it. We can't earn it by witnessing. We can't earn it with monetary gifts to the church. We can't earn it by living a goody-goody life. God's love is a gift, and God's gift to men is love.

I don't know why God loves me, and some of my friends—and probably some of my enemies, for that matter. But He does, despite our weaknesses and failures, and all any man needs to do is reach out and ask, believing he will receive. And the love and faith that is given to him is beyond anything that man can offer, and is never weakened by disappointment or discouragement, but strengthens him in everything he does and in every walk of life he chooses to travel.

And I would want my son to love his fellow man. The strongest love I've ever experienced is between football players on a team. Right from high school through professional ball—and I'm now associated with the toughest, roughest men in the world—I've always been aware of the great love teammates have for one another.

It's not "sissy" to love . . . to have deep concern for your fellow men and to want to help them and do your best for them. This is part of what makes the human life so wonderful. And it's something we need a lot more of in this world—understanding, communication, and love for one another.

My son would also discover that many men in his business or career, and I include athletics, have achieved success in their field without being professing Christians. But, when a man accepts Christ into his life, he is a better man for it and able to succeed better. He has peace of mind, love in his heart, and he has a special, calming strength that will make him a better athlete or ditch-digger or doctor. Accepting Christ may not make a man stronger physically, or a faster runner, or a higher jumper, or more skilled at his trade or profession . . . but just *knowing* that God stands beside you gives you a tremendous inward peace. It enables you to accept defeat and bounce back without too much self-recrimination, and without anger toward other people. It enables you to concentrate on those things which have to be done in order to turn a defeat into a victory, a failure into a success.

A man without God may rise very high in his chosen field. It will depend upon his ability, and upon the "luck" that follows him. But a man *with*

God will rise above his abilities, scaling peaks he could not even begin to climb were he alone and solely dependent upon his own talents. A fair football player who is dedicated to God and calls upon the strength of God to help him do his best, is preferable to me to a real hot-shot who might come apart mentally and emotionally when the game gets rough.

Finally, as I said in my talk before the Georgia State Jaycees, I want my son to play to *win* . . . in life as well as in his career. I don't play a football game to lose, or to tie. I play it to win. Businessmen don't work night and day to lose, or to break even. They work to make a profit and to win. This is the basis of our free society, and it should be the basis of everything we do in life.

In our sophisticated society today, our young people are often taught that it is more virtuous to lose gracefully than to win. But there isn't any virtue in losing! The end effect of such teaching is that young people will not be bothered by losing. They won't hurt inside, where it counts. And if it doesn't bother them, they'll be *consistent* losers.

The true competitor is hurt deeply when he loses. He acknowledges his defeat, but he convinces himself it is only temporary and he will come back, and come back, and come back, until he stands in the winner's circle.

We need sportsmanship, true, but let's not misconstrue sportsmanship to mean a casual acceptance of defeat.

Christ is the victory in life. Nobody wins without Christ—nobody. A man may accomplish every goal he sets out to achieve, but, in the end, if he does not have Christ—or if Christ does not have him—his work, and his triumphs, and his very breath have been meaningless and worthless. There can be no acceptance of defeat in this matter. Here, indeed, the game of life is played to win, and the devil literally takes the hindmost.

These are some of the things I would want my son to know, and the earlier he can recognize, and understand, and accept Jesus Christ, the more wonderful and fulfilled his life will be.

18

The Giants

Many people have speculated as to why I asked the Minnesota Vikings to trade me in 1967.

The reasons were personal, and very real to me. Sometimes the easiest course to take is the least controversial one—but it may be that neither course is the right one. Deciding was one of the hardest and toughest things I've ever had to do, but I felt for the good of everyone concerned it was the only thing to do. I could not return to Minnesota with a free and open mind; therefore it would have been unfair to the team, the coaches, and the management for me to return. I gave Minnesota six years of my life, and I'll always be thankful for those wonderful experiences, and for what everyone there did for me. I left something of Fran Tarkenton up there, and I wanted so badly to win an NFL Championship for the Vikings. But that desire will have to be carried to the New York Giants. Elaine, Angie and I leave Minnesota with wonderful memories and the assurance that we still have many lifelong, true friends in that great state.

In the 1966 season, the New York Giants had won exactly one game and had finished in the Eastern Division cellar. Fans' interest in the team had hit a resounding low, attendance was going down, and, to complicate things further, Earl Morrall, the Giants' starting quarterback, had broken his right wrist.

As a consequence, a major rehabilitation program was needed, and the first order of importance was to look for a quarterback.

In the winter of 1967, the Giants found themselves in an enviable position to make good progress in their comeback efforts. As part of the NFL-AFL merger, the Giants had been given special consideration allowing them to have the top pick in either the 1967 or 1968 draft for a college quarterback. They additionally had the option to trade that pick for a veteran professional quarterback.

When I announced in February, 1967, that I wanted to be traded, it opened the trade doors for the New York Giants. After a few weeks, during which other teams made their bids for my services, Jim Finks, general manager of the Vikings, and Wellington Mara, president of the Giants, closed the trading deal. Professional football is a business; the Giants had made the best offer to the Vikings, and the Vikings accepted it.

The trade included the Giants' first and second draft choices in 1967, the first draft choice in 1968, and another man to be traded at a later date. There were some alternatives to this arrangement, but, generally speaking, that was the sum of it.

Although nothing looked good for the Giants in 1966, they have a fine football team with great and near-great players. It's a young team that got the toughest kind of experience in 1966.

The most important part of the trade is that both the Giants and the Vikings got what they wanted. Mr. Mara happily signed the papers for the trade, and Jim Finks of the Vikings was reported to have said that it was a pleasure to do business with Mara and that both teams got the best of the deal . . . exactly as it should be.

As for me, I was happy and eager to join the Giants. It seemed like the old challenge all over again . . . a team on the bottom of the heap that needed help, lagging interest from the fans, predictions of dire prospects. . . . I'd gone through this before, and it sparked my interest and determination to do my part in building up a team that people were turning their backs on.

Furthermore, I couldn't help but be excited about the prospects of playing for a New York club. The New York Giants have always been respected as one of the most solid organizations in all sport. Also, New York City is the greatest pro football city in the world. My responsibility of influence also increases by going to New York; and again I ask for God's strength and love.

Right now, as I'm writing this book in the winter of 1967, I have yet to play my first game for the New York Giants. All of the events recorded in this chapter have just happened, and by the time you're reading these words I will have probably begun my 1967 season with the Giants. There will be some adjustments to make as I learn more about the talents of my teammates and the wishes of the coaches and management, and I'm sure that we'll field a fighting team in 1967, and an interesting and colorful one.

As far as I'm concerned, my goal is a Giant championship. I don't know how long it will take us to get on top, but I don't doubt for one moment that someday we'll do it.

And you can rest assured that in whatever way I can, through victory on the football field and in every other way possible, I will continually seek opportunities to glorify God.

One last word. Thank you, my friend, for giving me the opportunity to talk to you through this book. I pray to God that the testimony I've given here will be meaningful, and that each reader will put this book down feeling a little closer to Christ, and to the faith that has blessed my life beyond my ability to express it.

Go forward in faith—and *win!*

Epilogue

"New York City," so the saying goes, "is a nice place to visit, but you wouldn't want to live there." Much the same could be said of the New York Giant team that Fran Tarkenton joined in 1967: it was nice to be on a visiting squad coming to town for an almost certain victory, but it was no fun to be playing for the New Yorkers.

The once-proud and powerful Giants who took the Eastern Conference title in the National Football League for 1961, 1962, and 1963 were guilty of a collapse that was as sudden as it was complete. The very next season the Giants finished in last place, and the losses continued steadily during the next two years. Obviously, something had to be done.

The Giants tried to solve their problems by procuring a quarterback who could lead them, if not to the Promised Land, at least into the end zone often enough to make them winners again. On March 8, 1967, the Giants obtained Francis Asbury Tarkenton, who had been named after Francis Asbury, one of the first Methodist missionaries in the United States. New Yorkers—fans, the Giant team and its management—expected much from Tarkenton. He gave them plenty to shout about, game after game coming through with scintillating performances in which he blended accurate passes with his own special kind of dazzling, scrambling runs. Nevertheless, much as Francis Asbury the missionary encountered difficulties despite his numerous skills, so did Francis Asbury the quarterback find that his talents were otfen negated by his teammates' ineptness. Life for any quarterback wearing a Giant uniform in those days was positively dangerous. The Giants, if nothing else, were consistently incapable at all phases of the game as they stumbled, fumbled, bumbled, dropped passes and perpetrated transgressions unbecoming of professional football players. One of the most painful afternoons of Tarkenton's life came when, during a 25-3 loss to the Dallas Cowboys, he was sacked ten times.

Early on in New York, comparisons were frequently made between Joe Namath, the quarterback for the New York Jets, and Tarkenton. The conclusions of such observations were invariably the same: Namath was clearly the free-swinger, the blithe spirit; Tarkenton was the clean-liver in whom could be found no flaw of character. Finding that Tarkenton practiced the Christianity he had been taught and that he was sincere in his beliefs, the press accepted him for what he was. Throughout his five-year stay in New York, Tarkenton was treated with uncommon respect by the press. One of the many things about Tarkenton that caught the attention of the press was Fran's unashamed enthusiasm for football. Playing for a second-rate team did not diminish Tarkenton's hope that he could someday attain the pinnacle of football success: leading his club to a Super Bowl title.

"For athletes, the challenge is the thing," Tarkenton said. "Sure, we play for the money. We have to get paid, like anyone else. But there's also the challenge to go out there and test yourself. To play for a winner is not only a personal satisfaction. It is personal pride.

"One thing I object to in sports is the use of the terms 'winners' and 'losers.' I don't think there is any such thing as a loser. I play quite a bit of tennis, and I suppose there are 400 or 500 tennis players that I can beat back home in Atlanta. There are also another 100 players in Atlanta who can beat me. If I play only those last 100 all the time, does that make me a loser?

"Take Sonny Jurgenson. He's a great quarterback. But he's never played for a winner. Does that make him a loser?"

When it came to losing, Tarkenton had to endure more than his share of it while in New York. In addition to the defeats suffered on the playing field, Tarkenton admitted there were others he sustained when out of uniform.

"Bob Tucker [a tight end with the Giants] is my roommate on the road," Tarkenton explained in 1971. "When we're in the room we play chess or a game called Battleship. Bob has been beating me at Battleship. And when it come to chess, he *always* destroys me."

For the most part, though, Tarkenton's years with the Giants were notable for his virtuoso performances. In 1967, his first season in New York, he threw 29 touchdown passes, more than he ever had in any one year before or since. The following season he guided the Giants to a stunning 27-21 upset of the Dallas Cowboys. New York's first score that day came when Tarkenton, unable to find an open receiver, scampered 22 yards for a TD. Fran, who completed 16 of 24 passes that day, pulled off another strategic maneuver later in the game. Sensing that the Cowboys were preparing to have their linebackers blitz, he changed the play at the line, flicked a soft pass over the middle to Homer Jones, and then watched gleefully as Jones sped the rest of the way for a 60-yard scoring play.

In 1969, Tarkenton was selected as Sports Father of the Year, an honor that was topped off a week later by the addition of a son, Matthew Francis, to his family. Tarkenton threw five touchdown passes in a win over the St. Louis Cardinals in 1970 and shortly thereafter rallied the Giants for three fourth-quarter touchdowns to shock the Washington Redskins 35-33.

Before the start of the 1971 season, his last as a

Giant, Tarkenton became embroiled in a salary dispute with the club. On the eve of the team's first exhibition game that August, Fran walked out. Three days later he returned, signed the contract that had originally been offered him and contritely admitted to the press, "I'm very, very sorry it all happened the way it did. It seemed I was doing the right thing at the time. But now I admit it was a hasty move."

On January 27, 1972, Fran Tarkenton was traded again—back to the Minnesota Vikings. Unlike the Giants, who regularly yielded more than 300 points a season, the Vikings had a stalwart defense. In 1971 the Giants gave up 362 points, the Vikings 139.

Tarkenton's return to Minnesota occasioned numerous assessments of his career. Most of them were highly complimentary. What few detractors Fran still had harped on two items: he scrambled too much and his arm was not strong enough. One of the obvious dangers of being a scrambling quarterback is the increased risk of injury. Amazingly, however, Tarkenton has never suffered an injury of any consequence. What's more, he had played 153 consecutive games in the NFL before being benched during his finale with the Giants, who wanted to trade him and were not about to risk injury to their prize piece of merchandise.

As for those who complained that Tarkenton could not throw the ball as hard and as far as some other quarterbacks, his statistics offer their own reply: in 11 seasons he had completed 2,075 of 3,797 passes for 216 touchdowns and he already ranked fifth on the all-time list of NFL passers. Statistics also proved that his scrambling had paid off with 3,019 yards gained and 25 touchdowns.

On top of all that evidence, Tarkenton chose to say a few words in defense of himself and others who have been or will be similarly criticized. "Look at the top five all-time passers," he began. "How many of them have a real gun for an arm? Sonny Jurgenson, yes. But Len Dawson, no. Johnny Unitas, not really. Bart Starr, no. Me, no. That's just it: you don't *need* a gun. I can throw a football 61.5 yards. I have measured it. My arm is good enough.

"Many people in and out of the game really don't understand what it's like to be a quarterback. It's easy to second guess quarterbacks. I do it myself when I'm watching a TV game. But even the scouts don't understand the position. Look at the top five again. Jurgenson was a No. 1 draft choice, but Dawson was waived out of the NFL. Waived out! Unitas was a free agent when the Colts signed him. Starr was a seventeenth-round draft pick. I was a number three.

"All I ever hear about from scouts, though, is what a kid's arm is like. Well, you can scout his arm and his size and his intelligence. But you can't scout his leadership, or his ability to react under pressure, or his ability to make the right decisions—and those things are vital when it comes to quarterbacking.

"When you get to the age of 30 [Tarkenton was 32 at the time] and if you have been able to survive the crises, then you're really ready as a quarterback. Dawson was better after he was 30. So was Jurgenson. So were Norm Van Brocklin and Y. A. Tittle. When you get to be 30 you know the trouble spots, you know what you can do and what you can't do. Like me. I know who I am."

Tarkenton may have known who he was, but during his first year back in Minnesota, the Vikings seemed to forget who they were when it came to defense, giving up 252 points. In the 1973–74 season, though, with rookie running back Chuck Foreman joining the team and with Tarkenton hitting on a remarkable 61.7 percent of his passes, the Vikings won 10 of 12 regular-season contests. Then they stopped the Redskins 27-20 in a divisional playoff and disposed of the Cowboys 27-10 for the conference title. That meant that, at long last, Tarkenton had a chance to capture an NFL championship. Unfortunately, the Miami Dolphins throttled the Vikings 24-7 in Super Bowl VIII.

Tarkenton donated his entire $7,500 Super Bowl check to charity, half of it going to help retarded children, half of it to aid a drug rehabilitation program. Explained Tarkenton: "My cup is almost full. Sometimes I feel a little awkward when I meet and talk with people in need. I mean, I look at my own life and I have to say, 'It's exciting and good and prosperous.' I only wish I could have given $15,000. If this money can help salvage a life, then thinking about who won or lost the football game won't seem as important to me as I always thought it would."

Tarkenton and Minnesota both continued to excel the next two seasons, outscoring the opposition 687 to 375 while winning 22 of 28 scheduled games. Although Tarkenton was hampered by a sore throwing arm for much of 1974, the Vikings made it to the Super Bowl again, this time losing to the Pittsburgh Steelers 16-6.

Preparing for the 1975 season he indulged in one of his favorite off-season activities by going up to the attic of his house, getting down on his knees and throwing a football 20 or 30 times a day at a mattress.

Before the season began much was said and written about Tarkenton's accomplishments, about how he almost surely would go on to surpass every major passing record and how he would someday be inducted into professional football's Hall of Fame. Also brought up was the surprising fact that, despite his proficiency for so many years, Tarkenton had never been chosen as the league's All-Pro quarterback and that he had also never been picked as the best player in his own conference. Praise for Tarkenton came from many corners, as if there were suddenly a concerted effort to pay tribute to him for his years of on-field mastery.

"He's always positive," said Vikings center Mick Tingelhoff, seven times an All-Pro. "He never says, 'Let's *try* this.' It's always put to you as something that is going to work. If you play with him a while you learn he is going to come up with the big play."

Another Viking, John Gilliam, an All-Pro wide

receiver, said: "He knows what I'm going to do before I do it." That was Gilliam's way of trying to explain the almost magical way Tarkenton has of finding his receivers when none seem to be open for a pass.

Tarkenton has not been a prima donna, something that Minnesota coach Bud Grant has been especially thankful for. Said Grant: "Some quarterbacks can't throw in practice if it's windy or wet, and they have other hang-ups and quirks for other situations. But Francis never puts on airs. He's always there, always working. If you need an extra body for a kickoff drill, he'll jump in line. That sort of attitude has a beneficial effect on the entire team. Francis is never a doubter. He's always a doer. And now he has proved that he is the complete quarterback."

Opposing players also spoke highly of Tarkenton. Mike McCoy, a defensive tackle for Green Bay, summed up the feelings of many who have played against Tarkenton by saying, "When you have to face him you don't get much sleep the night before the game. He puts a lot of pressure on you with all that dancing and moving around he does, and you can never be sure where he's going or what he might do next."

Speaking about the records he seemed sure to break in the near future, Tarkenton himself said, "They matter, but only in the right context. They don't mean anything during the season. If I can reach them, I'll think about them during the off-season when I can afford a glow and an ego."

At age 35, Tarkenton had one of his finest seasons in 1975, completing more passes than he ever had (273 of 425) and passing with greater accuracy (64.2 percent) than ever as he connected for 25 touchdowns. One of his most satisfying performances came when he twice brought the Vikings from behind and took them to a 28-17 win over the Packers. Tarkenton was on target with his first seven passes that afternoon, with 16 of his first 18 and, overall, with 24 of 30 attempts for 285 yards and three touchdowns. A brief look at his three scoring passes that day represent a microcosm of Tarkenton's varied abilities. Tarkenton's first TD throw came off a play-action maneuver to the right side as he rifled the ball five yards to tight end Stu Voight. His second scoring pass came when he dropped back, floated a ball over a defender's arms and into the hands of John Gilliam in the end zone. The third score came off one of Tarkenton's scrambles. After zigging, zagging and bringing the 39..590..No Time for Losing Green Bay crowd to its feet by eluding assorted Packers, Tarkenton zipped a 10-yard pass to Chuck Foreman for another touchdown.

Tarkenton's hopes were high that, at long last, he and the Vikings could become Super Bowl winners. They never made it to the title game, however, suffering an improbable 17-14 loss to Dallas in a playoff game when Roger Staubach and Drew Pearson of the Cowboys combined on a desperation 50-yard scoring pass in the closing seconds. Shortly after the game Tarkenton received an even deeper shock when he learned that his father had suffered a fatal heart attack while watching the game at home on television.

With the season over, Tarkenton had time for "a glow and an ego." He could look back upon 15 NFL seasons, could reflect upon having set league marks for most career passes (5,225), completions (2,931) and touchdown throws (291). "The Scrambler" had also scored 28 times himself and had gained more yards rushing (3,629) than any quarterback in NFL history. And Tarkenton could take time to look at the trophies he had won in 1975 for finally being named to quarterback the All-Pro team and for being the league's Most Valuable Player. Perhaps, too, there were moments when Fran Tarkenton could ponder a statement he had made a number of times during his career: "I'm preaching a sermon when I play on Sunday." Yes, Tarkenton does "play" football. But he has done so with his own form of eloquence on the field and has conducted himself with such dignity in all phases of life that he has, in a very real way, been a living testimony to Christ.

The Publishers